Smouldering Fire

Smouldering Fire

The Work of the Holy Spirit

by

MARTIN ISRAEL

CROSSROAD · NEW YORK

1981
The Crossroad Publishing Company
575 Lexington Avenue, New York, NY 10022

Copyright © by Martin Israel.

Printed in the United States of America

Library of Congress Cataloging in Publication Data

Israel, Martin.
  Smouldering fire.

    1. Holy Spirit. 2. Spiritual life—Anglican authors.
I. Title.
BT121.2.I84   1981   231′.3   81-9794
ISBN 0-8245-0072-5   AACR2

*I thank Denis Duncan for his constant help,
guidance, and encouragement.*

The scripture quotations in this book are
from the New English Bible.

Contents

At each moment of time, in the fullest meaning of the word "now", Christ is born in us and the Holy Ghost proceeds, bearing all Its gifts.

(John Ruysbroeck)

What is soilèd, make thou pure;
What is wounded, work its cure;
What is parchèd, fructify;
What is rigid, gently bend;
What is frozen, warmly tend;
Straighten what goes erringly.
(From the thirteenth century hymn to the Holy Spirit,
Veni Sancte Spiritus, translated by J.M. Neale)

Foreword

THE THEME OF this book is the problem of good and evil and their reconciliation in Christ. At first I had the Holy Spirit in mind as the central focus for my meditation, and indeed the Spirit plays a primary role in the book as the agent of human advance to the knowledge of God. Since so many books on the Holy Spirit had appeared in recent years, most of them directly related to the Charismatic Renewal within the Church, I intended concentrating more on the psychological and psychical aspects of spiritual life, and indeed, these matters occupy a considerable part of the text. But as the work proceeded, it was shown to me that something more was required: the charting of the work of the Spirit in man from the birth of spiritual awareness to the ultimate confrontation with evil that brings with it personal death and the rebirth of a new person. The five crucial events in the life of Jesus — birth, baptism, transfiguration, crucifixion, and resurrection — are the paradigm of man's ultimate deification, and as such these have been the salient points of reference in this account of the work of the Spirit in human consciousness.

As the work progressed, much was shown me concerning the nature of the very limited reality of this world of toil and strife. The conclusion of the book was something I had not considered when I started writing: an analysis of the polarities of darkness and light between which both our mortal lives are suspended and the world grows, suffers, and ultimately perishes, and then of their ultimate reconciliation in a realm beyond mortal distinction and separation.

The theme is not a new one, but it needs to be restated in terms of the contemporary human dilemma.

Prologue

In the beginning of creation, when God made heaven and earth, the earth was without form and void, with darkness over the face of the abyss and a mighty wind that swept over the surface of the waters. God said, "Let there be light", and there was light. (Genesis 1:1-3)

To be born is to come to a knowledge of one's own independent existence. God created form out of the void so that He might love it and that in coming to its own self-awareness, it might reciprocate that love to its Creator.

People often speak of love as if it were an expression of cosmic benevolence directed in a diffused way at no particular person or thing. It is sometimes called good-will. Such good-will is deeply suspect because it affects to be benevolent and universal in scope, but fails to commit itself to a single finite action. In other words, real love is deeply personal. Eventually it extends its embrace to all people, indeed the whole creation, but it never allows any one person to be submerged in the sea of corporate humanity or any one thing to be swamped in the mass of the created whole.

God showed His love by His directive Word who ordered creation, and His out-flowing Spirit Who infused life into it so that it might progress under its own momentum, yet inspired by the effulgent energy of the Godhead – Father, Word of Wisdom, and Spirit of Life. When the creation was effected out of the void, which is the totality of the divine presence, time, as we understand it, began. It started with creation and ends when the creature returns of his own free will to the Creator, as perfect in love for Him as He is for His creatures.

"God loved the world so much that he gave his only Son, that everyone who has faith in him may not die but have eternal life." (John 3:16) This great statement does not refer only to that event which Christians call the Incarnation, but is a measure of the eternal gift of His Word that the Father bestows on the universe He has created. The Incarnation is to be seen as the supreme demonstration in mortal flesh of the eternal relationship that exists between Creator and creation.

"Then God said, 'Let us make man in our own image and likeness to rule the fish in the sea, the birds of heaven, the cattle, all wild animals on earth, and all reptiles that crawl upon the earth.' So God created man in his own image." (Genesis 1:26-27)

In the beginning the creation is scarcely aware of its separation from the Creator. It is only when the fully sentient creature, whom we call man, is formed, that a personal consciousness is added which can see itself apart from the creative process as well as at one with it. In the Creation story man himself is at first unaware of his separate identity from the world of bliss he inhabits. And there is no death. But at a certain stage in his growth it is decreed that he must learn of the principle of diversity that governs creation, so that he may begin to play his part in the exchange of love that energises the universe. Love, as we have already seen, is a willed exchange of devotion, that gives of its very essence between one individual and another. When there is primal union in which the one person does not so much as recognise his own identity as separate from the other, there can be no exchange of love from him to the other. This principle is seen in marital life whenever a child is born; the mother becomes aware of her offspring as soon as she sees it separate from herself and she loves it for itself alone. But the child cannot begin to reciprocate that love for many years, until it comes to a knowledge of its own identity and its relationship to its mother.

God, of course, knows His creation from the beginning, but the creature has little knowledge of Him. Man, at least in our little world, is the creature who has been given the supreme privilege of having so highly developed an intellectual and spiritual consciousness that he can aspire to a direct relationship with God. Man is, therefore, not only an animal but also a spiritual being – one in whom the Word of God is capable of speaking and the Spirit of God of acting consciously to awaken the whole world from sleep to purposeful activity.

And so it was man's supreme privilege to love God directly, and in so doing to reflect God's love on to the entire universe so that it too could grow into a knowledge of God's love and rise from the sleep of darkness to the life of plenitude. But man misused his knowledge. He learnt the nature of the principle of diversity that governs creation only too well, but instead of using the power that was given to him constructively for the raising-up of the world he used it divisively for his own selfish ends. Then did the knowledge of good and evil enter the world, with man heavily identified with the evil that diminishes creation and brings it back to the point of primal chaos, instead of leading it onwards beyond the darkness to the full light of God's love. This was the tragedy of the event that is called "the Fall". When man fell from union with God into conscious separation, time became an instrument of limitation, and man was imprisoned in a finite world limited by space and bounded by death. And he was destined to come to a full knowledge of himself in the suffering that is a part of living in a world of separation, removed from a direct knowledge of God.

This is the inner meaning of the Creation story told in the first four chapters of the Book of Genesis. Of course it would be not only absurd to relate this story to our scientific understanding of the creation of the world and the theory of evolution, that is accepted by all knowledgeable scientists, but it would also show a lack of that deeper imaginative grasp of truth that marks the height of human wisdom. What this biblical account of man's origin is attempting to penetrate is his relationship to the source of creation, which we call God, and his fall from that union to a separative, sinful existence. Although time commenced when the creation was called forth "out of the void", it becomes a conscious modality only when a creature is evolved who can be so aware of it that his life is centred on the demands it makes in terms of finitude and death. While in the vast universe of which we are now more fully aware than in the past, there may be myriads of intelligent forms that can work constructively with time, in our own world it seems that the human intelligence alone is so endowed. It is the limitation of the scientist's understanding of man that he can see the human race only as an evolving animal form with remarkably high intelligence based on an exceptional development of the brain. Another dimension to this view of human nature needs to be added: the infusion of the Word and Spirit of God into a physical form, or body, that is fit to receive it. This 'mystical' dimension of the human personality cannot be proved scientifically, but it is experienced daily in the lives of human beings and recorded in the annals of human sanctity that illuminate the history of all the great religious traditions.

At the end of the fourth chapter of the Book of Genesis it is recorded: "At that time men began to invoke the Lord by name." Religion, as we know it, is born as alienated man becomes aware of deity, separated by an immense gulf from him and yet closer to himself than his own soul. Religion is to reach its end in the New Jerusalem, where there is no temple; for its temple is the sovereign Lord God and the Lamb (the Word made flesh Who has redeemed man from his separative existence and reconciled him to his supreme calling as a Son of God). The entire journey of humanity from bestiality to divinity is spanned in the vast prospect of biblical imagery.

1

Birth — Natural and Spiritual

Then the Lord God formed a man from the dust of the ground and breathed into his nostrils the breath of life. Thus the man became a living creature. (Genesis 2:7)

THE SPIRIT OF God infuses all living creatures. Man in this respect is no different from any other living being. The body is created out of the material of the earth from which it is fashioned by an artifice so marvellous in its complexity and yet reliable in its uniformity that when a flaw does occur, we are all shocked by it. The Word effects creation, and is in the creature. The Spirit infuses the creature with life. By this life the creature is made capable of progressing by experience in a medium of time through the limitation of space.

This is the world of becoming, in which all creatures are to experience their own identity in a dimension of limitation and finitude.

It is unfortunately true that many people appear to function at so low a level of consciousness that the seat of identity, which may be called the ego or the personal self, does not play a real part in any of their actions. Most actions are really unconscious responses to outer events and inner drives that impinge themselves on people, and the end of the action is simply the achievement of immediate comfort. In the case of many individuals, there is an awareness of the body only, but no communication with a deeper essence within it. However, when one makes a conscious decision, no matter how shallow and selfish it appears, one is at least responding to the core of identity, the personal self. A person is one who reacts consciously from this independent centre of identity and is prepared to follow the call of that centre in faith. The person is truly born when he is able to make an independent decision and act on it.

To come to the knowledge of one's true identity, which is equivalent to affirming that one has a unique, priceless essence to give the world, is a process that should begin very early in life. The infant first comes to know its value because its parents acknowledge it and love it for what it is, although it can give nothing in return — except itself. Though in its present state it is helpless and a source of inconvenience, it is also a being of infinite potentiality. As soon as it is accepted as a person, it can begin to explore its own personality and find that it is a focus of unique presence. To accept a person as he now stands is to start the process of his own self-recognition. Admittedly this self that is recognised is a fragile thing, depending for its support on the good-will of the outside world, seen primarily as the family. But it is an important beginning.

To be centred in the self is necessary for survival, let alone effective being. The satisfaction of the desires of the body for comfort is a paramount feature of a child's life. If the body is given its due acknowledgement with acceptance and love, the child will accept the physical part of his make-up without the embarrassment or the exhibitionism that is a feature of a poorly integrated personality. And the child will also begin to grasp that its identity extends beyond the confines of the body, which at the same time is in no way diminished in his estimation, for it is the essential ingredient of his life on earth. And so it comes about that, as a person grows into adult life, his identity is based on both his physical integrity and his growing mind.

But even this is not the end of our growth into identity. One's sense of inner presence must be such that is can withstand the blows of outer fortune. Whereas the child's sense of identity is fragile, depending on the approval and acceptance of those stronger than itself, when an individual comes more fully to himself, he has to make decisions that may estrange and even antagonise those closest to him in blood ties. This is where the moment of willed choice, of crisis, is so important. When this decision is taken and acted upon, the person affirms himself and sets out on an independent course in life. This course may appear to be extremely ill-chosen and have disastrous effects in the short term, but no matter how short-sighted his vision, the participant in life has at least left the shores of stagnation and entered the turbulent waters of experience.

A real decision always has moral overtones; the question of what is right or wrong in terms of the individual's well-being and his relationships with those around him becomes increasingly important. When the person begins to see his identity as a point not only confined to himself, but as an aspect of the community in which he lives, he is coming to a deeper appreciation of himself and is venturing into his spiritual inheritance.

The experience of individual identity is one's first taste of reality. As the experience of individuality becomes more extended into an awareness of communal identity, so does the understanding of reality grow in comprehensiveness until personal identity becomes increasingly irrelevant except in the context of fellowship with others. It is through the Spirit of God that growth into individual awareness and its expansion into communal identification becomes possible. Man becomes his full self when he is one with the Spirit of God that informs the spirit within him.

Although the Spirit of God is always within man, being the very flow of life that courses through his body, human consciousness in its natural state is seldom aware of that Spirit. The individual begins to know the impact of the Holy Spirit when decisions of a moral nature impinge on him, and he has to make conscious choices, which by the very nature of the circumstances are bound to alienate others whom he holds dear. When the Spirit is pulsating through a person, he is no longer asleep to reality; at last he knows that his life has a meaning and a purpose that transcends the merely evanescent satisfaction of the physical senses.

"It is time for you to wake out of sleep, for deliverance is nearer to us now than it was when we first believed. It is far on in the night; day is near." (Romans 13:11)

That which awakens us from the somnolence of inertia to a realisation of the self is the Holy Spirit. As a person grows into life, so he becomes increasingly responsive to the call of the Spirit, a call that directs him on a far journey away from simple thoughtless conformity with the life around him to a path of hidden promise, to the experience of a new realm at once unknown and infinitely desirable. The call may lead him through terrible dangers and almost insurmountable difficulties, but the strength of the self within, impelled by the Spirit of God, will ensure a final victory. This victory will not necessarily be a worldly or an intellectual one; it is a victory of the spirit of man over the flesh that anchors him to a present situation of impotence, so that the flesh may be informed, transmuted, and glorified to that spirituality which is the stuff of eternal life.

What is the relationship between the spirit of man and the Holy Spirit? They are not identical, at least in natural man, yet neither are they totally disidentical. The spirit in any living organism is the power within it that drives it forward into the unknown. In the more primitive forms of life, this movement is activated by the physical desire for survival and procreation, but were it not for the power of God within even the lowliest organism, that humble form could not survive, let alone renew itself. The very means whereby our physical body does undergo renewal, for instance in the healing that occurs after an injury, is the pulsating spirit of God within each component cell. Medical skill can put the body in the best situation for healing to occur, but it cannot induce, let alone command, the individual cells to perform their wonderful work of division, migration, and differentiation that is the heart of the healing process.

This, to me, is in its own way, as marvellous as any miracle recorded in the Bible. Indeed, the difference between a

healing miracle and the normal healing process is essentially
one of time. What occurs in the space of days or weeks under
normal circumstances seems to take place with remarkable
rapidity, or even instantaneously, in a healing miracle. It
would seem that when the Holy Spirit is in conscious control
of the creature's life, He can effect in the "twinkling of an eye"
what He would normally take a considerable time to fulfil,
and what indeed might be completely thwarted by a perverse
attitude on the part of the creature.

If this insight is applied to the relationship between the
spirit of man and the Holy Spirit, it would seem that, in the
natural man, the Holy Spirit infuses the personality as an
unrecognised host, and that the power of life He bestows is
dulled and distorted by the adverse current of psychic
elements in that personality. Thus the life that the Spirit
bestows is crippled, wasted, and made awry by the destructive forces of the psyche. Its power is used selfishly, and its
effect is impure and adverse. Yet without the power of God
man would not be able to act even perversely. It is good to
realise that all action, no matter how destructive it may
appear, is ultimately under the creative Word of God and
subject to His control. "You would have no authority at all
over me," Jesus replied to Pilate, "if it had not been granted
you from above." (John 19:11)

But what about the individual who has been denied proper
recognition at an early age? And what about those who
through unfortunate circumstances of upbringing have been
the victims of unconscious complexes which have interfered
with their proper psychological development? How can these
types of people develop a sense of their own identity? They
may instead identify themselves with their past unhappiness,
or even fail to attain any conviction that they count for
anything at all. While acknowledging the necessity for skilled
psychotherapeutic help in many such cases, I would emphasise that even such unfortunate people can attain full personal
identity, and this not only in spite of their psychological
crippling but because of it. The life of full spiritual knowledge is sometimes more readily attainable to those who have

been wounded or even crippled emotionally than to those whose lives have known little internal stress or disappointment.

The reason for this apparently paradoxical situation is basic to the nature of inner reality. I may accept my importance as a person by virtue of the loving acknowledgement I have always received. But this sense of importance may easily lead me to complacency, indolence, and increasing self-centredness at the expense of other people. In the end I might regard myself as the centre around which the world was meant to revolve. On the other hand, if I am crushed and left utterly bereft of all outer support, the true self may be the only focus of reality left to me, and I may start to know who I am in the deepest humiliation.

It has been a source of constant delight to see people whose early lives were one tragedy of neglect and suffering, and yet who have faced the challenge of inner authenticity and become whole as a result of it.

There are some people who resign themselves to misfortune so that they retreat from life and fail to become real persons, while others, admittedly a minority, faced with similar circumstances and scarred with much suffering, come to a knowledge of their real worth. These are among the leaders of mankind. There seems to be a fundamental attitude of life-acceptance in the few and life-denial in the many. The ones who fail life's tests sink into a pit of self-pity and despair. Those who pass the test of suffering come to an understanding of inner authenticity, and never cease to be aware of the amazing fecundity and potentiality of life. This prevents them becoming enmeshed in regrets and reproaches; instead they get on with the work of living. Temperament is often invoked as an explanation for the differing responses of people to the blows of fortune. But the heart of the matter is the personal response to the ultimate factors of existence, and these are illuminated by the Spirit of God within the individual.

A life that is blind to the transcendent reality that underlies the world of common life is enclosed in the mortality of transience; everything has its moment of perfection and then fades away into annihilation. Life ends in a whimper of disillusionment and self-pity. A life that looks forward to all experiences — the unpleasant as well as the pleasant — as part of growth into a full person with enhanced usefulness to the world, ends in a realisation of inner identity. To put this in a more religious perspective, those who are open to the Spirit of God, whether in success or in failure, are given the inclination and the courage to press onward to the great quest: the knowledge of God and the attainment of the stature of a real person.

It can therefore be said that the experience of identity in a realm of limitation is the way of growth. Growth is the very purpose of life, and death in turn is the end of a particular phase of growth. By an act of faith we believe that the creature may venture through death into an unknown country where he may come to experience more of his identity in other dimensions of limitation.

Birth has, then, three components. There is firstly the *physical* birth of the body that succeeds its existence in its mother's womb. Then there may be *personal* birth at a time when a decision of moral urgency is made that determines the future life of the individual. This decision gives the individual his first experience of autonomy, his first assertive action made independently of his parents or mentors. Finally there is to come the *spiritual* birth, when the impress of the Word of God acting through His Spirit informs the person of his true identity, that of a Son of God. This is the birth of the Word, identified as Christ in the Christian tradition, in the soul which, for convenience, can be defined as the true essence of the person, of which the personal self, or ego, is its manifestation in the outer world. But whereas the ego is a fluctuating centre of awareness, the soul, or spiritual self, is immutably fixed as the centre of the person, and grows into the knowledge of God (and of itself) through the Spirit, which in turn is centred within it.

The Word lies dormant in the soul like a seed, to which many Christian mystics have compared it. Its moment of germination is the moment of spiritual birth. Then the person *knows* his destiny.

2
The Birth into Spiritual Awareness

The hand of the Lord came upon me, and he carried me out by his Spirit and put me down in a plain full of bones. He made me go to and fro across them until I had been round them all; they covered the plain, countless numbers of them, and they were very dry. He said to me, "Man, can these bones live again?" I answered, "Only thou knowest that, Lord God." He said, "Prophesy over these bones and say to them, O dry bones, hear the word of the Lord. This is the word of the Lord God to these bones: I will put breath into you, and you shall live." ... I began to prophesy as he had bidden me, and as I prophesied there was a rustling sound and the bones fitted themselves together. (Ezekiel 37: 1-7)

THIS MARVELLOUS ACCOUNT of the resurrection of the body of the people of Israel, crushed under Babylonian captivity, is also the way of spiritual rebirth for the individual. The paradox of birth is that it always succeeds death. To put this even more starkly, one has to die before one can know God. The Spirit descends only on him who has either given of himself to the highest that he knows, or on him who is so crushed by calamity that he has of necessity been shriven of everything by which he had previously identified himself. Even the birth of a baby is the moment of its separation from the warmth and security of the mother's womb. To live is a dangerous experience, because it is always hazardous to move into the unknown future. But he who takes the plunge soon discovers that he is not alone. The Spirit of the God without knocks at the inner door of the soul and is accepted in trust and thanksgiving.

I knew a man whose life was selfish and hedonistic. For one thing he had far too much money when he was young. He not only spent it improvidently but he valued everything, even friendship, by the price of the object or person. Relationships were, for him, a means of self-gratification, and yet he had considerable charm and a deceptive inner warmth which attracted many people. His marriage soon foundered on the rocks of infidelity, and he came to realise in middle life that, despite his affluence and his physical attractiveness, he was desperately lonely. To escape from an encounter with himself, he would seek every possible and available activity. Some of his exploits were mean and sordid. And yet, strangely, he did have an inner warmth which made the more perceptive observer hope that eventually he would come to himself and start to do the work for which he was called. The crisis came when he was in his late forties, for then severe mental disease struck him. His family history was bad, since a number of relatives had also suffered from mental illness; indeed his early, feckless behaviour was probably a presage of the later breakdown that was to scar him so severely.

As he languished, so his life collapsed about him. His wealth was dissipated while his family melted away, and his associates — none was worthy to be called a friend — moved elsewhere. The only people who cared about him were the medical and nursing attendants, and these were so severely overburdened with other duties that they could not give him as much attention as they would have liked. He had no religious faith, and little awareness of his own identity apart from the outer appurtenances of money, sex and frivolity that had previously sustained him.

In his anguish, he had an experience of being separated from his body and seeing his life pattern from a great distance. Indeed, he was given a panoramic view of his past life. He saw how a pall of selfish hedonism had thwarted any good that he might have done, and how few traces of noble actions punctuated the sequence of his existence on earth. A voice then asked him when he was going to start the work he had come in to do. He had never been in the least interested in religion, but at last, bereft of all conceit and in fact experiencing a heightening of consciousness that spoke of the proximity of physical death, he knew intuitively who was addressing him. The voice was at once inside him and part of the universal world. It was the voice of God's Word, the Christ, which could at last make itself heard as conscience when the clamour of personal assertiveness had been stilled by illness and annulled by impotence.

The medical attendants ascribed this psychic phenomenon to the disease itself, but the man knew better. As one gropes for truth in a dark fog of despair, so one becomes emancipated from conventional theories expounded by professional authorities. "Where the Spirit of the Lord is, there is liberty" (2 Corinthians 3:17) — we shall come to this theme on more than one occasion later on. This man knew that the focus of truth deeply set in the universal consciousness of life pulsating within him was the light that alone would heal his broken mind and set in action his growth into a real person. To the amazement of all concerned, he steadily improved, was able, in due course, to relinquish the drugs prescribed for his condition, and started to do the work for which he was called. This was to care for others and be a support for the needy. He came progressively to a mature religious faith, and the latter part of his life was singularly blessed with good works.

This sequence is reminiscent of the most famous parable of Jesus:

"There was once a man who had two sons; and the younger said to his father, 'Father, give me my share of the property.' So he divided the estate between them. A few days later the younger son turned the whole of his share into cash and left home for a distant country, where he squandered it in reckless living. He had spent it all, when a severe famine fell upon that country, and he began to feel the pinch. So he went and attached himself to one of the local landowners, who sent him on the farm to mind the pigs. He would have been glad to fill his belly with the pods that the pigs were eating, and no one gave him anything. Then he came to his senses." (Luke 15: 11-17)

We know the Parable of the Prodigal Son well enough, but the important facet that concerns us here is the moment light descended into the derelict heart of the foolish young man. The Spirit of truth which leads all creatures into truth is available to the humiliated and broken man, and at last he begins to see the light. This light shows itself to him as hope, one of the greatest gifts of the Spirit. Meaning is suddenly revealed in a singularly aimless, selfish life, and the broken, yet now wise man can return to the source of his being in faith, albeit a faith heavily overlaid with feelings of guilt and unworthiness. But the most revealing part of the Parable of the Prodigal Son, and also of the life history of the man I have described, is the wilful movement of the hero from the security of conventional propriety and religion. It is this wilful movement that marks the authentic birth of the individual, even if his path starts on a downward slope of sensuality and folly. It would seem almost as if the Spirit within the person impels him to relinquish comfort and conformity and proceed on an ill-starred adventure to attain integrity of the personality. When one compares the Prodigal Son with his brother who stayed at home, or the mentally broken man with his more successful peers, one cannot but exalt the first over the second. Although these latter may appear to be much more successful and desirable in the world's eyes, they lack that understanding and compassion which come only from a deep identification of the personal self with that of the other individual in his greatest travail.

The moment a person comes to himself, facing the reality of his own responsibility, is the moment of birth of the Spirit within him, or rather, the Spirit of God has entered his personality and is attending the birth into consciousness of the Inner Christ, that Word of God deeply implanted in the soul as a vibrant seed. It follows therefore that the Spirit acts primarily to renew, resurrect and sanctify the consciousness of the person. Only when that Spirit has become a conscious reality in the life of the person does he have a real conception of his own identity. When one knows what one is doing and is aware of what one is attempting in the wider context of life, one is at last imbued with a conviction of inner authenticity, that what one is and does is of real importance, not only to oneself but in the broader concern of the world. Conversely, the person uninformed by the Spirit is rootless and his life lacks ultimate meaning. This does not mean that a Spirit-filled life is one that necessarily proceeds along well-defined tracks and ends in material success and prosperity. The Spirit may lead the aspirant into a maze of unexplored passages, each of which has something to tell him. But the main feature of a directed life is that even when one appears to be completely lost, one is still impelled by a sense of purpose within that shows itself outwardly as hope and expectation.

The action of the Holy Spirit in informing and renewing consciousness, like all actions of the Spirit, cannot be induced by the will. Techniques, by their selfish attitude, serve only to occlude the Spirit, Who comes to the hungry as pure grace. "Thus speaks the high and exalted one, whose name is holy, who lives forever: I dwell in a high and holy place with him who is broken and humble of spirit, to revive the spirit of the humble, to revive the courage of the broken." (Isaiah 57:15)

The Holy Spirit is sometimes described as the feminine principle of the Trinity. This is, of course, a symbolical description, for the Persons of the Trinity all combine the male and female principles of a new creation. In Jesus Christ Himself, though masculine in outer form, there is the coinherence of man and woman that is the true mark of a celibate, the one who can love all humanity in complete identification with the lowliest as well as the most exalted. Nevertheless, the fertilising power of the Spirit, His attendance on the birth of Christ within the soul of man, and the nurture that He gives to all creatures so that they may attain nothing less than the stature of spiritual reality (which is eternal life), is of the nature of female generosity and providence rather than male assertiveness and leadership. The Spirit, in other words, by His courtesy, infuses us and renews the powers inherent in us. He does not take us over and direct our lives for us. Any power that over-rules the human will and forces itself on the person cannot be divine.

Free choice is the divine gift to man. As he grows into maturity, so the way of the Spirit opens itself to him, and in the end it shows itself as the only way to authentic living, but at no time is man forced to accept the Spirit. He can remain in his present situation indefinitely, until he realises that he is, literally, in hell. At that point he will accept the Spirit gladly. But when the Spirit is accepted, responsibilities are thrust on the person, and life begins in earnest. Gone is the ease of careless living; the birth into the Spirit is the beginning of the encounter with the Living God, Who demands nothing less than perfection from His creatures. And this perfection is to realise in living form, the divine image in which man was created.

3

The Consecration of the Will

For though many are invited, few are chosen. (Matthew 22:14)

INDEED, THE CALLING to God's service, or to spiritual illumination — the two are in essence alike — is for all men. This is, literally, Everyman's vocation. There is no one, at least among those who are proficient mentally and emotionally, who has not received the call. I believe, too, that there is a call even for those who are so retarded mentally that they cannot achieve independent life in the world around them. The inner identity, the soul, probably registers many experiences which would appear to be beyond the grasp of the rational mind.

If, however, everyone receives a personal call to higher service, why are there so few who stay the course? Jesus says: "The gate that leads to life is small and the road is narrow, and those who find it are few." (Matthew 7:14) To find this road to authentic life is hard: it requires dedication of the self to the exclusion of all lesser concerns, perseverance in spite of all disappointments, and self-giving service to others without the expectation of any recognition. Yet it is not we alone who make the decision: it is the Holy Spirit without, making Himself ever more clear to us within, that begins the purification of our soul and the forming of our will. As I say, we are all called by the Holy Spirit from afar. Some do not respond at all; indeed, they do not experience spiritual birth.

Some would like to respond, but do not have the inner resources to withstand the temptations of the world around them. A few are prepared to make the great decision and embark on a life of privation in the face of plenty, to traverse a solitary path at a distance from their compatriots, to experience the destruction of their most cherished possessions in the hope that the one real possession we all have in common may be revealed to them.

Why is it that only a few people in any generation appear to be selected quite specially for spiritual illumination, while others, the great majority of mankind, grope haltingly on the path of life for some meaning to their existence, for some purpose in the daily round of trivialities that symbolise worldly existence? The fact of election cannot be denied. Just as some people are born with remarkable artistic, intellectual, or psychical gifts, so there are those also who are natural mystics. For these people nothing suffices but the vision of God.

Looking at this on a superficial level, it would seem to be monstrously unjust that the few are vouchsafed a full vision of authentic life, perhaps at a very early age, while the many do not seem to be participants in the race to spiritual understanding, so obtuse is their sensibility and so limited are their aims in life. But this is a very narrow approach to the problem. In fact, the spiritually aware person has to learn that the vision of God is attained only by the painful process of fully incarcerating himself in the material of this world, so often stinking and corrupt, so that every part of his personality is given its due and can attain its own mastery. He has to essay the depth of human degradation as well as the heights of mystical ecstasy. He has, in fact, to translate the primal vision into the facts of life, so that life itself may attain eternal significance by his witness.

Furthermore, the spiritually obtuse person is not necessarily destined to remain in a state of somnolence for ever. He too is to awake and confront reality:— "Awake, sleeper, rise from the dead, and Christ will shine upon you." (Ephesians 5:14) As he is shriven progressively of all the possessions with which he identified himself, so he too will come to know the source within him that is the only real, enduring possession, which, paradoxically, he shares with all other creatures. It is a consoling thought that although sanctification is almost impossible to envisage, so high is it above our imagination, it is nevertheless within the grasp of all people, no matter how undistinguished and unpromising they may appear to their fellows. By contrast, great artistic, intellectual, and psychical skills are, by their very nature, the gifts of only a small number of people. They cannot be acquired by the majority of people, who are well advised to cultivate their particular talents instead of yearning for gifts which are quite clearly not within their compass. But great skills are also a potential snare, for unless used for the greater good of humanity, they can, all too easily, separate the practitioner from his fellows and also from God. Self-inflation is one of the greatest hazards in the proficient life. As one marvels at one's own proficiency, so one begins insidiously to deify oneself and lose fellowship with the source of all creative action, the Holy Spirit.

What then does election give us? It makes us eligible to bear the suffering of the world. It allows us to participate a little in the redeeming sacrifice made by the supreme man, Jesus Christ, so that the messianic age, inaugurated on the Cross and proclaimed by the Resurrection, may, after two thousand years of travail, be finally established in the world. I repeat, one is elected to bear the privilege of Christ's suffering. This is not a comforting thought, but it is a strengthening, invigorating one. It gives purpose; it lends compassion; it promises glorification not only to oneself but to the whole world.

The reverse side of vocation is commitment. This is the true baptism experience, and its prototype is the baptism of Jesus at the hands of the forerunner, John the Baptist. The hidden years of Jesus surely were a preparation for the ministry ahead of Him. Likewise, His baptism at the hands of a very remarkable man, but a man nevertheless, was a submission of Himself to the demands and frustrations of the uncomprehending world. And in the act of humble self-giving He is found worthy to do the great work. "And a voice spoke from heaven: 'Thou art my Son, my Beloved; on thee my favour rests.'" (Mark 1:11) At the same time the Spirit, like a dove, descends upon Him. Only when the will responds directly and ungrudgingly, can the Holy Spirit fully enter the soul as a consciously directing power. As I have already indicated, the Spirit is present in all creatures; in man there is the potentiality for the Spirit to be consciously acknowledged and proclaimed. The time at which this happens is the moment of his birth into the Spirit. But only when the soul responds fully to the power of the Spirit, saying as Isaiah did after his vision in the Temple, "Here am I, send me," (Isaiah 6:8), can the Spirit dwell fully in the soul and influence the spirit of man which is deeply set in the soul. Thus it is said, "The Lord shines into a man's very soul, searching out his inmost being." (Proverbs 20:27) When a conscious decision is taken to work for the coming of the Kingdom of God, the Holy Spirit is as fully active in the soul of the disciple as He is outside that soul. He has taken his dwelling-place in the midst of us, and we are called by His name. (Jeremiah 14:9) This is the priceless fruit of spiritual dedication.

The Holy Spirit starts the regeneration of the person first by enlightening his consciousness and then by consecrating his will. The call to service is made real only when there is a positive response to it in full dedication of the personal life. Then the person has himself chosen, and is participating actively with God in the life of spiritual reality. This is the reason why many are called, but few are chosen: only those who choose a way of self-sacrifice to a realm that is glimpsed in faith, believing that this way is nevertheless the only one that can bring with it authenticity in living, can in turn receive the divine blessing and the downpouring of the Holy Spirit upon them. This way may require a complete renunciation of all one's past life and associations for the supreme quest of unitive knowledge. But more often one is called on to pursue the old life and associations with a new awareness of the reality that underlies them, so that the common round and the daily task may themselves be illuminated with the vision of eternity. To me, this is a particularly glorious way to establishing the Kingdom of God on earth, which is the ultimate meaning of the Incarnation, both of Christ and of Everyman.

The baptism conferred by the Holy Spirit confirms one in the spiritual life and confers with it a strengthening of the will and the beginning of an integration of the personality. It can occur only in a person who is, at least temporarily, cleansed of sinful pride, who has already passed through a minor death with Christ, and is now raised with Him to at least a glimpse of the Father's glory. In this way his feet are set upon the new path of life, as St Paul writes. (Romans 6: 3-4) The Sacrament of Holy Baptism, usually performed in infancy, is a presage of this passage from death to life which should in fact be a daily occurrence in the life of a spiritual person, although there are, of course, exceptional episodes in which everything he had held dear may have to be denied so that he may know the centre of eternity within himself. In fact when one's will is consecrated to the great work, one has to bid farewell to one's past life in order to proceed unencumbered by old habits and thoughts. This leave-taking has a poignant quality, like that of a grown son bidding farewell to his parents as he makes his way to a new and forbidding country. The sadness is felt mutually by the son and his parents, but he must not look back, once he has "set his hand to the plough." The Kingdom of God is not attained by reverting to past attitudes of mind, or by returning to childish dependence on others. This is the death of a past way of life. Only when one has broken loose from the imprisonment of sentimentality can one begin to relate to the past constructively and lovingly. True love thrives only in an atmosphere of freedom where self-giving is effected without the necessity of support or even recognition by the other person.

There are many in the field of spiritual endeavour who, while longing for enlightenment and the experience of the abundant life, refuse to commit themselves to any particular spiritual discipline. They remain spectators in the field of life, weighing up various philosophies and religious systems with sympathy, evaluating different schemes for personal development, and often supporting them verbally. But they do not become personally involved. They prefer the label of reverent agnostic to membership of a finite religious group. Many such agnostics admit they envy those who have manifest faith, but clearly, by the witness of their lives they have no ardent wish to taste that veritable faith for themselves. Until they do commit themselves to a definite scheme of religious training, however, they will never know the faith.

Faith is a gift of the Spirit. Through it we aspire to heights of endeavour far beyond our evident ability. But it is we ourselves who have to put that God-given faith into practice by doing the great work. God will not do it for us. However, once the task is attempted and its travail borne, the Spirit can at last take His place in our midst, in the soul, and be our guide through the inevitable planes of adversity and darkness until we know final release and triumph.

The Holy Spirit makes His presence felt within us as joyous faith. This is not a feeling of personal confidence that could easily boost the personality, but one of an inner assurance that goodness lies at the heart of reality, and, that, as St Paul says, the sufferings we now endure bear no comparison with the splendour, as yet unrevealed, which is in store for us. (Romans 8:18) Thus the fearful faith, that allows us first to offer ourselves in God's service, becomes a mighty paean of self-dedication in faith, for the coming of His Kingdom. It is this type of faith that is one of the gifts of the Spirit enumerated in I Corinthians 12:9. It is the faith that saves.

This is the essential difference between the agnostic purveyor of spiritual truth, no matter how much good-will he may pour forth, and the fully dedicated person who chooses the way to authenticity, even when all the auguries around him are unfavourable. There is a world of difference between good-will and the will to good. The first is a kindly attitude; the second commits that attitude to action by living the good life. But this life is less easy than might be imagined. For once the will has been consecrated to God's service, it then has to be reformed and transfigured, so that, from being an expression of personal desire, it becomes the instrument of God's work. No wonder it is more comfortable to remain on the side-lines and simply watch the drama of life from a safe distance, while shouting slogans of encouragement to the participants in order to assuage one's own conscience.

I have tried to show how the Holy Spirit is our true guide to the abundant life. Not infrequently He comes to us when we seem to be in safety and comfort, as He did to the Prodigal Son, and urges us to wake up and be about our business. Our first movements may horrify our friends and colleagues as no doubt did the improvident actions of the Prodigal Son. To those watching us, all may seem a tragic waste of time and energy. Indeed, we may have to taste the bitter fruit of utter degradation, as do some who tread the paths of occultism and witchcraft. We may have to face the personal disintegration that sometimes follows any abuse. And yet, despite all this, there is infinite hope for us. Once we have learnt our lesson thoroughly, the Spirit becomes available to us once more, reminding us of our high calling as sons of God, and leading us back, chastened but no more mere children, on to the authentic path to God. By this dire sequence of experiences, we will have learnt to distinguish between the gold of spirituality and the dross of materialistic glamour and occult power. We will also have learnt important qualities of the inner life of other people, at last being able to relate to them in warm compassion. As a result of this, we can start to identify ourselves with the pain and woe of many of our fellow human beings.

When we have faced the sinful side of our nature, the side that exalts what we believe to be our self-interest to the detriment of the wider concerns of our fellow beings and of God, we may begin to know the reverse side also, the side that speaks of the potential glory that lies within the heart of us, and indeed of even the most unpromising person. It is only when we have the courage to face corruption within ourselves that we can be purged by the refining fire of God's love. Thus it was with Isaiah in the Temple, who could at last say, "Here am I, send me."

At that moment of absolute commitment the Holy Spirit descends on us, claims His own within us where He had always been though previously hidden from us, and starts His transforming work on our personality.

The point of first encounter is the will.

4

Descent into Darkness

Jesus was then led away by the Spirit into the wilderness, to be tempted by the devil. (Matthew 4:1)

THIS IS THE true sequel to spiritual dedication: the disciple is then exhaustively tested in the furnace of truth. The Holy Spirit, as the farewell discourses of Jesus state quite openly, is the Spirit of truth, who guides us into all truth. He does not speak on His own authority, but tells us only what He hears. He also makes known to us the things that are to come. (John 16:13) The will, already consecrated, must not be hindered and perverted by impulses coming from the unconscious part of the personality. It is a great gesture to give of oneself fully for God's service. But how much of this dedication is play-acting? How much of it is a spectacular ritual designed unconsciously to release one from the sordid facts of one's worldly situation? How much is it a way to attract the attention of one's fellows and become a centre of admiration? How much is it a calculated attempt to acquire psychic power with which to dominate other people? If we were aware of our inner life, we would know that these false motives are unconsciously with us even when we appear to make the decision that is morally right and spiritually inevitable.

Turning for a moment to Jesus Himself and the temptations He underwent, we have much to learn about the nature of man, even divine man. It is stated, almost without reflection, that Jesus was like us in all points of humanity except that He was without sin. The sin of which we all partake is an exaltation of our own interests above those of other people; of this I have already written. But Jesus must have been vulnerable to the inroads of sin, otherwise His victory over the demonic forces of the world would be such a foregone conclusion as to be mere play-acting. If He is true man, He must be subject to all the temptations that litter the path of Everyman. He must, in fact, be responsive to demonic elements as are other men. It is His response to these elements that is distinctive.

The devil who plays a central part in the temptation drama can be interpreted in diverse ways, and indeed all of these interpretations shed some light on the truth and can be usefully combined to produce a composite picture. The demonic is primarily within us. We know it as the subterranean force that would lead us to destructive actions against others and ultimately even against ourselves if it were given free rein. It is generally quiet when all is going well with us, for then morality pays, and the status quo is what we desire most. But as soon as our security is threatened, the demonic within us is unleashed with the greatest ferocity and it attacks the person who threatens our ease. It spits out in venomous jealousy at anyone who seems to have gifts superior to our own. It will stop at nothing to demean his abilities and diminish his reputation by subtle calumny and calculated innuendo. It saps the faith of the innocent and works for the complete destruction of all that is noble and beautiful. Its essence is nihilism. The devil is in essence the spirit who denies. No wonder Jesus is reported as teaching that whosoever is a cause of stumbling to one of these little ones who have faith in Him, it would be better for that person to have a millstone hung round his neck and be drowned in the depths of the sea. (Matthew 18:6) We all have this in us, so much so that we cannot begin to know who we really are until we have faced this terrible reality.

But the origin of the demonic is not merely personal. It is part of the principle of divisiveness that rules the natural world. The origin of evil, which is personified as the devil, can be laid at the realisation of his isolated identity, which came to man early in his self-awareness. It is doubtful whether evil as such is a part of nature until man himself has evolved. To be sure, each animal strives for itself and its progeny, and will not shrink from using the weaker creature for its prey. Its predatory nature, however, is limited, and the strong animal shows no tendency to be wilfully destructive. In man, the free, rational will can lead either to the vision of God or else to such bestiality that a psychic residue of enormous emotional power is left after the event. An unappeased person can emanate such vicious hatred that total destruction of his fellows may follow if his actions are not curbed. The several examples of genocide in our own allegedly civilised century are only too obvious a demonstration of this tendency. It would seem therefore that the dark core present in the human psyche is one with a psychic emanation of destructive nihilism that is cosmic in scope and related in all probability to the "powers and principalities" in "high places" of which Paul speaks. These are the angelic forces known only to those of us who are psychically attuned.

One cannot, however, come to this attunement with powers that are external to one until one is in communion with similar powers within oneself. In the psychic realm the within and the without, though separate, are also in indefinable continuity, like the seamless coat that Jesus wore when He was crucified. (John 19:24) Furthermore, the destructive, cynical element that questions our faith and is our adversary is also the means of our final liberation from the thralldom of illusion. In the great parable of Job, were it not for the temptation of the devil which he successfully parried, Job would never have seen God with his own eyes. He would have remained a sincere, conventional religionist! In this story the temptation that has been withstood is despair. In the life of Jesus the temptation is self-aggrandisement by the use of psychic power conferred, at least potentially, by the power of the Holy Spirit. And openness to that temptation is mediated by privations consequent on the ascetic life of withdrawal into the wilderness.

The wilderness is always the place where we have to face reality, for it is there that we are completely alone. Even those dearest to us cannot accompany us, since they would be repelled by the squalor of Job's desolation or totally bewildered by the isolation of Jesus' unique endurance. And all who tread the path of full personal development are co-heirs of Job's dereliction and Jesus' human loneliness. Although He was one with the Father, He had nowhere to lay His head in true fellowship with those around Him. They had no conception of the man whom they thought they knew.

The purifying power of silence is terrifying. In it we can no longer escape from the reality of ourselves by means of the trivial surface conversation that passes for relationships in everyday life. A silent retreat in the fellowship of like-minded companions brings one dangerously close to one's true identity, and what confronts one is seldom attractive. The silent isolation into which the Holy Spirit leads us after the dedication we have made to God is, however, terrifying in its starkness. We have no shred of vesture to conceal the grime within us — resentment, jealousy, fear, and selfishness. This is because, when we are left completely alone, these destructive attitudes and emotions, usually well-hidden behind a facade of worldly interests, now emerge and reveal our inner corruption very clearly. The trend of our thoughts when we are in total isolation is a clear indication of our spiritual state of being, and this is confirmed by the searing honesty of our dream life.

It is unfortunate that this aspect of the work of the Holy Spirit in our lives is seldom dilated upon, and is therefore woefully misunderstood. Instead there is more often the rather naive belief that dedication of the self to God automatically brings in its train peace, prosperity, and happiness. In some instances these benefits do show themselves in the short term, but it is important that they should not continue too long. Christ, though the Prince of Peace, comes, like the prophets before Him, with a sword. His first work is to cut away illusion; this takes the form of a comfortable, conventional type of religious observance and morality. On the surface this seems to be unobjectionable, indeed praiseworthy, but it has the unfortunate result of equating worldly success with spiritual growth, at the same time identifying failure and disappointment with unconventional religious or social attitudes. A dependence on the good things of life fosters a static view of reality. It does not encourage that adventuresomeness in living which is essential for the development of a fully integrated person; his gaze is averted from the truth within him to the success outside. This success may have to wane before the claims of inner authenticity can be faced with courage.

The reason why Jesus successfully withstood the temptations of the dark forces of the world around Him was not because He was indifferent to the power that was offered Him. It was because His soul was in personal relationship with His Father, so that of Him it could be said, "My Father and I are one." (John 10:30) When the love of God is the eternal radiance of one's life, the power of that love can never be deflected inwards to oneself; it is radiated outwards to one's fellow creatures. From this we can see that the inspiration of the Holy Spirit does not, in itself, guarantee that His power will be used profitably by the person on whom the Spirit descends. It can as easily be used unwisely and selfishly. This again is something that requires deep thought. The growth into spiritual maturity takes time and requires the experience of life. Our first encounter with the Spirit of God brings us to a new awareness of reality, but it requires much travail before that awareness is made substantial in our earthly life. Before this can happen we have to confront the dark, shadow side of our psyche. Having confronted it, we have to accept it, and wait patiently on God in the silence of prayer for healing to begin.

There is no short cut to the spiritual life. On the contrary, it is in accepting all the adverse qualities of our character in calmness and trust that we may come to know and accept other people also. In the spiritual life, the last to arrive are as welcome as those who seem to have been there from the beginning. Difficulties are not removed by the selfish will

intent solely on communion with God. They are removed by
the grace of God working silently within us when we are
empty of conceit and striving, and have given ourselves over
to God completely in deep prayer and service to the world.
There is indeed only One who will accept the negative,
destructive part of ourselves as readily as He welcomes our
admirable qualities: God accepts us as we are and, through
His love, teaches us to accept ourselves and our fellow men
also. Only then can redemption and salvation take place.

The wilderness experience is with us throughout our whole
life. There has to be a progressive transformation of the
personality. As we grow into spiritual awareness, so there is a
greater exposure of the depths within us. In these depths there
is heroism as well as cowardice, disinterested love as well as
selfishness, intuitive judgement as well as obtuse insensitivity.
No part of the internal life can remain hidden; every aspect is
brought out to the light of truth.

The process of healing that is such an important part of the
work of the Holy Spirit is based on this acceptance of the
darkness within, and this continues in even greater intensity
as insight deepens. Suffice it to repeat at this stage that, when
the Holy Spirit emerges from within the person as a conscious, directing element in his life, He leads him downwards into the bowels of his own personality, so that he may
know his present situation. Once this initial truth is fully
assimilated, healing becomes available and transfiguration
possible. The Holy Spirit does not lift one outside oneself and
from the place in which one lives into a realm of rarefied
spirituality in which all one's problems are miraculously
solved and a new life begins. On the other hand, He sets one
more firmly in one's proper place than ever before, exposing
all one's inner weaknesses and outer difficulties. But He gives
one the power to work with God towards the redemption of
those forces that are hostile, towards the spiritualisation and
glorification of all that is corrupt and debased both in one's
character and in the world.

Remember also that the true disciple is always in the
wilderness. He has to be there in order to support the

brethren as well as to be the guardian of the true doctrine. "Alas for you when all speak well of you; just so did their fathers treat the false prophets." (Luke 6:26) By this I am sure Christ did not mean that it is the duty of the spiritual disciple to antagonise his fellows gratuitously. Indeed, he should be an instrument of peace and healing. But by his witness, his very presence in a situation, he arouses the jealousy of those who seek high spiritual honours for themselves. His integrity, even if he is as silent as the suffering servant of Isaiah 53, is a constant reproach to the hypocrisy and superficiality of the masses. The Spirit of God arouses the antagonism of the spiritually blind so that they would stop at nothing to quench that Spirit. Therein lies the tragedy of our world, but in facing it with courage and faith, it can be lightened and relieved.

The spiritual path leads us through darkness. At times there are triumphs and great successes, but below the surface a brooding chasm yawns. Jesus knew that He had come to set fire to the earth, and how He wished it were already kindled. He knew He had a baptism to undergo, and He suffered under the constraint of patience until the ordeal was over. (Luke 12: 49-50) This final baptism comes at the moment of crucifixion, which does not take place until the aspirant is ready for it. Before that time he is prepared for this ultimate renunciation by the purging fire of the Holy Spirit, which ensures that no selfish impulse can separate him from God. When this has been done, the mortal ego transcends itself to attain the fullness of the spiritual self, which is of the stature of eternal life. At the same time selfish desires are transmuted into constructive attitudes of mind, concerned less about one's own benefit and more about that of one's fellows.

The work of the Holy Spirit in regenerating the unconscious mind by redeeming deeply hidden complexes is the basis of the healing process. Until we know what corruption lies deeply within us, we cannot accept it, and give it to God for the healing which He knows is appropriate for us. Authentic spiritual exercises lead us to that basic and sometimes forbidding knowledge. It is then that the agencies of healing, all directed by the Holy Spirit, can become active in our life.

5

The Regeneration of the Personality

Salvation has come to this house today! — for this man too is a son of Abraham, and the Son of Man has come to seek and save what is lost. (Luke 19: 9-10)

THE ROLE OF the Holy Spirit in regenerating the diseased personality so that its split-off, warring components can be integrated into a complete working unit, is one of the most important aspects of the spiritual life. It is also a dynamic point of operation between the work of the psychotherapist and the spiritual director.

As in all other aspects of human toil, there is always a living relationship between the human will and the power of God that comes to us as His Spirit. The human will acting alone cannot effect any creative illumination, nor can it reclaim a lost person or a broken life. On the other hand, the Holy Spirit does not act in a situation where the will does not co-operate fully and unreservedly with Him. I am sure this was why Jesus did not work many miracles in Nazareth, where there was a lack of faith. The people there knew His background too well to be impressed by Him and so allow Him to work among them. (Mark 6: 1-6) Faith in the healing power of God does not require a simplistic credulity any more than theological orthodoxy. It demands a simple openness to the uncharted magnanimity of God, Who accepts us as we are in perfect love, and then, with our co-operation, begins

the regenerating work on our personalities. Until we understand the nature of this personal regeneration, we can never
come to grasp the meaning of spiritual healing.

The range of human personality is vast. There is, at one
pole, the brute beast, no different in appetites from his
animal cousin but vastly more dangerous because of his
intellectual development. At the other pole, there is a
disinterested search for truth, a weary toil demanded by the
creative impulse, a self-sacrifice on behalf of his fellows that
comes near indeed to the Incarnate Christ. St Paul in
Romans 7: 21-25 contrasts these two polarities, the first
identified with our bodily nature and the second with the
Spirit of man, and he sees that, in all men, these two natures
are constantly in conflict. The difference between the self-
centred person and one who is spiritually dedicated lies in the
altered balance of power between the two, but in no one can
the first be eliminated by the second. To come to a full
realisation of the spiritual potential within us, we have also to
come to terms with our animal inheritance, not with resignation or even calm acceptance, but with joyful recognition.
Until we can face the whole range of our personal response
with equanimity, there can be no real healing in our lives,
and therefore we will be unable to comprehend the full extent
of God's love for us. It is not often realised how spiritual are
the animal desires that are common to all of us. Indeed, our
animal brethren often appear to emanate more natural grace
than do anxious, alienated human beings.

Without our animal inheritance we would neither live nor
actualise our potentialities on this earth. Without the direction of the spirit within, we would never transcend our
own endeavours and would remain in a state of inertia. The
spirit in man urges him to surpass his past records whether
athletic, technical, or intellectual. But when this spirit is consciously infused by the Spirit of God, the will to transcend is
no longer limited by personal objectives; it becomes universal in scope and sympathy. As St Augustine puts it: God
has made us for Himself and our souls are restless until
they rest in Him. But can my defective, sinful soul find that

rest in Him Whose perfection is too great for me to contemplate? St Paul, at the end of Romans 7 says, "Miserable creature that I am, who is there to rescue me out of this body doomed to death?" And he finds the answer, "God alone, through Jesus Christ our Lord." (verses 24 and 25)

What does this mean in practice? One thing is clear to me: a mere theological acceptance of the saving power of Christ, no matter how sincere it is on an intellectual level, does not in itself lead to any noticeable integration of the personality. On the contrary, the clinics of many psychotherapists have been filled by broken, sincere Christians who have been brought up from their childhood on a doctrine of their absolute unworthiness. Jesus is seen to be so good as to be scarcely human at all, and He has sacrificed Himself to save sinful, worthless mankind, yet mankind is still as corrupt and worthless today as it was long centuries ago. A monophysitic Jesus Who is divine but not human actually separates man from God, and cannot bring the healing of Jesus to His brothers in the flesh.

How did Jesus redeem those who were lost? He started by coming down to their level, by walking among them, and identifying Himself with them. Neither the prostitute nor the venal tax-gatherer was too debased to be close to Jesus. He sat among them and ate at their parties. Each Christian has a special text dear to him, and mine is Luke 15: 1-2: "Another time, the tax-gatherers and other bad characters were all crowding in to listen to him; and the Pharisees and the doctors of the law began grumbling among themselves: 'This fellow', they said, 'welcomes sinners and eats with them.'" And then follow the stories of the lost sheep, the woman who loses a silver piece, and finally the incomparable Parable of the Prodigal Son. You may be sure that Jesus loved the company of these people. If He had attended their parties and revelry with an air of condescension, pious disapproval, or evangelistic fervour, He would never have been invited a second time. He did not exhort the revellers to think about the deep things of life or to consider the fate of their souls. He seems to have reserved this important reflection for those who were ambitious for this world's wealth at the expense of their own authenticity as persons. This included even His disciples. (Mark 8: 34-38)

He loved the sinners of this world for what they were. They knew in their hearts how far from their true nature they had slipped. The woman who prostituted her body for a lust she, in all probability, did not share really hated that body. The tax-gatherer sold his respectability for money, which alone afforded him a sense of security that his upbringing had denied him. And Jesus accepted them with love and thanks-giving for what they were. As I have said, He put no demands on them before He associated with them; in doing that He alienated not only the traditional religionists of His time, but also the followers of John the Baptist, that stern, prophetic reformer who had no truck with dissimulation or hypocrisy, but was not notable for his sense of humour. This gift runs through the ministry of Jesus, although it is usually hidden from those who preach the Gospel.

An instance of this ironic humour, relevant to our present consideration, was His comment: "It is not the healthy that need a doctor, but the sick; I have not come to invite virtuous people, but to call sinners to repentance." (Luke 31-32) It was, alas, those who were full of their own virtue, who paraded their moral health, that were sick unto death, because they did not know themselves. Their moral rectitude and religious piety had separated them from the springs of life which flow from the Creator Spirit and are transformed by the human soul into warmth, fellowship, and love. By contrast, the established sinners against the moral order had scraped the depths of degradation and came to realise their unity, even if it was only a oneness born of depravity. Yet Jesus accepted them for their authenticity. And they saw in Him, with the vision of a child, a person who was a proper man. By His very presence, He not only challenged their present mode of life, but, far more important, He showed them the way of release from their thralldom to the flesh to a full realisation of their whole personality.

The beautiful account of the conversion of the tax-gatherer

Zacchaeus (Luke 19: 1-10) emphasises this. Jesus had merely to acknowledge this man who was hated by the crowd for his dishonesty, and to dine with him, for a radical transformation of his character to occur. Jesus rejoiced at his change of heart, but at no time did He judge or condemn his past life, any more that He did that of the woman taken in adultery. (John 7:53 — 8:11) He came to heal, or save (the two words are very closely linked), not to judge, still less to condemn. It was the actions of both the sinners and the pious religionists that condemned them. Whereas the sinners had the humility, in the face of Christ, to repent and seek salvation, the religionists were merely threatened by that same face. It showed them all too clearly the gulf fixed between their faceless conformity to the law (which they breached at every opportunity by casuistical hypocrisy so as to put themselves to as little inconvenience as possible, as Matthew 23 so starkly relates) and the law of love that alone can fulfil the moral law.

The prerequisite for the healing wrought by the Holy Spirit, as demonstrated fully in the ministry of Christ, is a wholehearted acceptance of what we are now. If we cannot face our inner dereliction, or those qualities that rob us of communion with our fellows, or those perversions which shame us so deeply that we cannot bear to face them in full awareness, let alone confide them to others who might help us, we cannot bring them to God for healing. This is the heart of the most deadly of sins, pride. A proud person is so enclosed in himself that he cannot accept love. And not accepting love, he is equally unable to give love to others. It often happens that pride has its origin in a deep, wounding betrayal at any earlier period of life, so that the person bears the painful memory of rejection and remains shut in on himself; he cannot open himself to the love of God. Until that memory is healed, there can be no regeneration of the personality. The great spiritual law is, "Ask, and you will receive; seek, and you will find; knock, and the door will be opened." (Matthew 7:7) But there is an inbuilt resistance to asking, a resistance based on our very proper feelings of unworthiness. We are indeed unworthy by human standards, yet supremely worthy by divine standards simply by virtue of God's love in creating us.

What we cannot face cannot be brought to God for healing. We approach the Father through the Son (now ascended in glory with the Father) and the Spirit of God infuses us, starting the process of inner healing. The essential spiritual insight that has come to me over the years is that God loves us as we now stand. Every defect, every weakness, every perversion is as much under the control of God and His glorious love as are the spiritual gifts we value. How often does one encounter a sincere, questing seeker, trying desperately to lead a Christian life but thwarted by some deep-seated defect, very often one of sexual aberration! His efforts to live in purity and dedication to the highest are shattered by the lust of the flesh within him. Or it may be a resentment so ingrained that it casts its malign shadow over the beauty of life and spoils every treasured memory. How can God face such a person? His life is a betrayal of all he believes with his mind and affirms with his lips. And yet God loves him precisely because of his weakness, just as Jesus loved the pariahs of society who crowded together to hear him. He Who makes the sun rise on good and bad alike, and sends the rain on the honest and the dishonest, Who sustains those who deny Him as well as those who love Him, can never, by His own nature, reject any of His creatures. It is only we who can reject Him, and in so doing we isolate ourselves from the lifegiving power of His Spirit.

God is not primarily rejected through the mind; atheistic intellectuals are often rejecting an image of God that is false, but have not the imagination to penetrate beyond that childish conception they so rightly despise. Those who really reject God often, paradoxically enough, affirm Him intellectually and in their words and worship. But their heart is far from Him because it is sealed and remote. The cement that shuts the heart is a combination of guilt and pride; it also occludes their spiritual vision so that they cannot see their neighbours either. If only they were able to see properly, they would soon discover how much they share in common with those around them: fear, isolation, anxiety, despair. Truly it is these negative attributes that bring us close together. This thought in itself gives us some insight into the value of a defect in our personality, once it can be faced, acknowledged, and given its due of love.

But how can I love something aberrant, unclean, and disreputable within me? By seeing it for what it is: a split-off part of the personality that is still of childish stature, and, being isolated, claims its due attention. As long as it is rejected, it will war with the remainder of the personality, violating any inner peace, and separating me from full attention to the present moment. As soon as it is accepted and cherished, I at once humble myself and bring myself into communion with those around me, who, as I have already said, are just as sick in soul as I am. To be sure, their weaknesses may be of a different nature to mine, but they produce a common disintegrating effect on the life of the person, leaving him a mere shadow of what he might have been had he the courage and faith to accept the difficulty, and work constructively with it. "Anyone who wishes to be a follower of mine must leave self behind; he must take up his cross, and come with me." (Mark 8:34) I believe the cross we, each in our own way, have to carry is that circumstance which prevents our life being successful, which takes away our inner happiness and security, which casts its shadow and leaves its pall of doom upon us. It may be a difficult personal relationship, ill health, a defect in intellectual development, or some inner moral weakness. We may pray for its removal, but not the slightest change will occur until we have contended inwardly with the difficulty.

Jacob was not a very admirable man when he was assailed by an angelic presence during the night. He had tricked his brother Esau out of his inheritance and had later been obliged to flee from his kinsman Laban. He was in a state of fear as the time of meeting with Esau drew near. But despite his ambivalent nature, he did not lack courage, and he contended with the angel of the Lord. He neither cowered in fear nor submitted with pious abnegation of self. In the end, despite a hip injury, he prevailed and would not let go until he had obtained a blessing.

Like so many inspired stories, this can be interpreted on many levels, but one thing stands out: Jacob is the representative of us all. When he faces the consequences of his sins and does not retreat behind plausible excuses or fulsome cajolery, he rises to the stature of a full man, one who strove with God Himself. (Genesis 32: 22-32) His subsequent meeting with his brother was amicable, and his name is raised to that of an immortal.

We each have some inner defect to confront, not with abject shame but with passionate affirmation. Once this thing of darkness which is within us is acknowledged openly, without deceit and without apology, it can be transformed. The transformation that culminates in healing may be rapid and painless, but more usually it is prolonged and causes much suffering within. The Holy Spirit brings a knowledge of truth with Him, and he incises the shell of a damaged personality until all the defective parts are exposed and acknowledged.

In our wrestlings with the dark forces within us, we can today count on the help of modern psychological understanding. We know how the will is undermined by subterranean complexes of high psychical potency, deep in the unconscious realms of our personalities. Modern psychotherapy is aided by the increasing understanding of the social and economic dimensions of sin. We now realise that we are as much sinned against by our environment and those who were responsible for our upbringing, as simply sinning ourselves. These insights help us to attain a wider view of the inadequacy that is part of the sinful world into which every soul is conceived. Well did the Psalmist write, "In iniquity I was brought to birth, and my mother conceived me in sin." (Psalm 51:5) It should hardly need to be said that sin has nothing to do with the act of procreation but is an inveterate part of the psychic atmosphere into which each soul is introduced at the moment of conception. And yet both Jeremiah and Ezekiel discountenance the old saying, "The fathers have eaten sour grapes and the children's teeth are set on edge." (Jeremiah 31:29 and Ezekiel 18:2)

The law of personal responsibility is not abrogated by the fact of communal involvement in sin. It tells us of the infinite worth of the person despite his inevitable contamination with the stain of the world. Indeed, it is only by the individual's growth into the likeness of God that some of the stain may be removed, that the evil in the world may be purged, and that the universe may be re-created in the pattern of God's excellence. "See that you work to the design which you were shown on the mountain." (Exodus 25:40)

Where does the work of modern rational healing agencies such as psychotherapy end and the inspiration of the Holy Spirit begin? The answer is, of course, that whatever work is undertaken to relieve pain or dispel ignorance is inspired by the Spirit of God. Every scientific discovery, every philosophical insight, every human aspiration that yearns for truth is due to the inspiration of that Spirit. But rational healing is applied from outside the person. It aims at disclosing the chaos within to the conscious gaze of the person, so that he may gain understanding of the deeper springs of his present infirmity. Such understanding helps to dispel feelings of guilt and releases him from a self-inflicted isolation. At last he can see how much in common he has with others and that his own inner pains are not unique. In diverse ways these patterns of suffering are repeated in the lives of all people. Yet all this intellectual knowledge may not, of itself, effect the slightest change in the inner attitude of the person. He can enjoy rationalising it to the extent of boring his friends with his psychological expertise, but inwardly he may remain as far from his centre as ever. Healing comes like a thief in the night, unheralded and unprepared, when a sudden change of heart is felt and the darkness of the past is lifted. Then at last the person is released from the imprisonment of childish ways of thought and outdated attitudes of mind, and he begins to reflect on his life clearly, perhaps for the first time. The emergence of the Spirit is sudden, authoritative, and incontrovertible. It unlocks the person's inner life, and he becomes less closed in on himself and more ready to open himself up to the love and the wounding of his brothers. The Spirit effects this opening of what was previously shut and inaccessible by the power of love. This love binds the broken personality, and sets in motion the transformation of all the unhealed elements within it. The Spirit is the heart of all healing, the centre of the process of restoration to wholeness. But it cannot be ordered from a distance, nor can it be attained from within until all selfish striving for mastery had been rejected.

It can therefore be deduced that only when a person has the honesty and courage to face the shadow within himself, and, at the same time, the faith to present himself fully to God as a living sacrifice, will the Spirit enter his life both as a gift from without and as a burning presence in the depth of his soul. It is the proof of God's unreserved, unquenchable love for him, and if for him, for all creation also. The Spirit is also the cosmic presence by Whom each individual grows into the stature of a real person, with Jesus Christ as the end as well as the promise of that perfection.

To summarise, it can be said that the regeneration of the personality is the heart of the process of healing and is the central work of the Holy Spirit in our lives. He makes us aware of the aberrations within us, gives us the courage to face them and accept them as integral parts of our nature, and fills us with the intuition of God's love for us as we now stand. In this way we do not need to divert our gaze from any aspect of ourselves, and can stand naked once more before our Maker as did Adam and Eve before they committed the act of insolent pride, exalting themselves above God, and separating themselves from Him. In this trusting nakedness, our essential beauty is once more revealed, so that even those aspects of our personality which were previously perverse and shameful are now within reach of God's grace. And then they are transformed into something beautiful and holy. This transformation is aided by all the healing agencies available to us, but the act itself is supernatural, being divine in origin. To be receptive to this Spirit that regenerates the personality, the pre-requisites are honesty, courage, humility and faith. It may take years before the incubus within is removed, but even during this period of waiting, one's sympathies are broadened and one can become an ever more useful servant for others. Our wounds become the agents for healing once we have transcended both self-pity and self-abhorrence, and have come to identify ourselves more with other people.

It is worth remembering that this process did not even really begin in the lives of Jesus' disciples until their Master left them on their own.

6

The Spirit as Healer

The written law condemns to death, but the Spirit gives life. (2 Corinthians 3:6)

HEALING IS THE binding together of the disintegrated personality into a new, transformed whole. Healing results in a true wholeness of the person which allows him to approach the transcendent holiness of God in intimacy and love.

We have been considering how the Holy Spirit regenerates the personality by infusing its dark recesses, brought courageously into the light of truth, with His power, so that what was formerly a source of shame and secrecy can now unfold into its true nature as a part of the creation of God. This is the beginning of the healing process and also its heart. The true Spirit works from within outwards. As the soul is cleared of the debris that occludes the Spirit within it, so the mind is sharpened and cleansed, and the body invigorated and renewed. The Holy Spirit is the power that integrates; He does not concentrate exclusively on one part of the personality, leaving the remainder without care. In this respect He differs from all the secondary agencies of healing, whether medical, psychotherapeutic, or psychic, which apply themselves predominantly to one part of the personality.

This means that the Spirit acts slowly and progressively. But what about the healing miracles ascribed to Jesus and His disciples? These surely were rapid if not instantaneous.

And were the people involved really healed? As far as the scanty scriptural record tells us — and we know little of their subsequent progress — they were cured of various diseases and infirmities. But cure of a physical or mental disability is not to be equated with healing of the personality. Jesus Himself, on more than one occasion, warns the person not to sin any more. If the healing had been complete, this warning would have been unnecessary. The person could never have returned to past inadequate ways of thought. But Jesus did not come to effect miraculous changes in people by intruding into their private lives and forcing them to turn to God. He knew and respected the integrity of every person He encountered. He wanted a free response acting by means of an informed, renewed will. He did not come to take people over by dominating them. His healing ministry was primarily one of spontaneous compassion, as for instance in the cure of the leper described at the end of the first chapter of St Mark's Gospel. He also healed to teach some important spiritual truth, as in the story of the man with a withered arm (Mark 3: 1-6), where He demonstrated that acts of compassion took precedence even over observance of the Sabbath. His healing power and miraculous acts were, furthermore, a demonstration that the kingdom of God was close at hand, which was the Good News from God that He proclaimed right at the beginning of His ministry. (Mark 1:15) He showed the way to the kingdom but He never forced people to enter it. On the other hand, He taught that the road that leads to life is hard and its gate narrow, and only a few find it. (Matthew 7:14) The Spirit Who proceeds from the Father and the Son is the life giver, but no one is obliged to receive the life He brings. Jesus came so that men might have life, and have it to the full (John 10:10), but no one was ever coerced into accepting Him.

When Jesus performed His healing ministry, He gave the afflicted their first experience of God's love. They were afforded their first glimpse of the Kingdom through the person of Christ and His act of divine compassion to them. Not all responded even if they were cured of their illness; in the instance of the ten lepers, only one returned to give thanks to God (Luke 17: 11-19), while the others took the gift for granted, and were as unhealed in themselves after their encounter with Jesus as before. But of those who responded in gratitude to Him, how many stayed the course and supported Him during His passion? Even His disciples ran away then. It was the later events of the Resurrection and the downpouring of the Holy Spirit that continued the healing initiated by Jesus while serving on earth. When their end was near, as often as not in martyrdom, they bore witness to a healing of the whole person that was of a different order to that started by the Incarnate Lord. Until the healing wrought by His Spirit is seen in this radical context, the Ministry of Healing will be a truncated, impotent thing.

When Jesus performed His healing work, His two great sayings were, "Your sins are forgiven" and "Your faith has cured you." Forgiveness and faith are the foundation stones of healing. They are complementary parts of the inner humility that is a prerequisite for receiving the grace of God. Faith is a state of being open to life's potentialities; by it the righteous man will live. (Habakkuk 2:4; Romans 1:17) It is not to be identified primarily even with a belief in a personal God, since some images of God are so dangerous psychologically that they fill the afflicted person with fear, guilt, and a sense of such utter unworthiness that he cannot begin to accept any healing or love. There is a close connection between faith and our ability to make relationships with others — our fellow men, the world around us, and the unseen hosts of eternity. I cannot begin to relate to anybody until I have a solid basis of personal identity. Until this has been attained, I will drift helplessly and never be able to perceive the concern for me of those around me, let alone yield myself to God's personal love. Faith is a giving of oneself in trust to the process of life, to the cosmic flow that orders all things aright. As I proceed in the venture of life, so I will come to a deeper knowledge of myself, light and dark elements mixing to form an intricate mosaic of personality. The knowledge, and the bringing together of the pieces of the mosaic, is given to me by God's love through the power of His Spirit. This is the way in which the injunction "Ask, and you will receive; seek, and you will find; knock and the door will be opened" (Matthew 7:7) is fulfilled. As I become more open, more trusting, and less enclosed, so the Spirit enters me from without and radiates within me.

This faith has nothing to do with a blind, compulsive belief in the personality of anyone (including even God, seen in a personal mode), or in some system of metaphysics, or in an occult power. It is rather a relaxation of the entire personality in the warmth of life, admitting my own ignorance but at the same time affirming a belief in my supreme importance in the scheme of things. As I wait in quiet expectation, so the strengthening warmth of the Spirit infuses me, and I begin to glimpse something of the nature of God in my life. He strengthens me and fills me with the courage to proceed in life's quest for healing. I repeat: there is no necessity for positive thoughts in this process. One need affirm no principle nor proclaim any system of belief. All that is needful is to be empty of personal conceit and to give of oneself unreservedly to the life of that moment.

What one receives in this act of childlike openness is beyond description. It is an encounter with the Living God, Who comes to us in a personal mode of being, so as to emphasise to us the supreme value of persons.

The forgiveness of sins is a natural result of the faith that will not shrink from exposure of the self to God, "to whom all hearts are open, all desires known, and from whom no secrets are hid." Of course He knows, but how often we play a private game of hide-and-seek with Him, pretending that we can deceive or dupe Him into condoning a false action! All we are doing, in fact, is deceiving ourselves. When we can face our diseased nature in full unashamed honesty, He can enter our lives in the form of His Spirit and show His eternal love for us. The forgiveness of sins at once removes all feelings of guilt. It goes beyond rational explanations or clinical analyses of past circumstances. It is as spontaneous as the joyous welcome given to the Prodigal Son by his father, who asked no questions and made no demands.

As we are forgiven, so a new principle enters our lives, the supremacy of love. We are now moved in our actions neither by fear nor a sense of duty but by such an overruling concern for others that only their well-being matters to us. In other words, the forgiveness of sins does not annul the consequences of sin. On the contrary, only when we know we are forgiven can we start to put right the damage caused by our past selfishness and thoughtlessness. And this new approach to relationships with others is not obsessive in intensity so that we overwhelm them with our guilt-ridden concern; it is calm, peaceful, and benevolent so that a feeling of trust can develop between all the people concerned. I am convinced that this is the pattern of growth in the purifying life of the world to come. The risen Christ, by His atoning sacrifice for the world's sins, raises the consciousness of all who are open to His love so that a real change of heart and mind, a "metanoia," occurs. Then we can start to atone for what was imperfect in our attitudes to the world and to our brothers. It follows therefore that faith makes us open to God's unreserved forgiveness, and the fruit of this is a changed response to the world, which is made manifest in good works. Works that come directly from the personal self are inevitably tainted with selfish motives, such as the need for recognition, the will to dominate others (allegedly for their own good), and the assuaging of feelings of guilt over past actions. This is true even when the works in question seem beyond reproach. But when works proceed from undemanding love for others, a love that has a divine origin, they set in train a sequence of benefits that bless giver and receiver alike. For then there is the divine-human collaboration which is the pre-requisite for all fruitful action.

This matter of divine-human collaboration is of vital importance in understanding the healing work of the Holy Spirit. He acts as a mediator between two or more people. He is the very basis of a loving relationship. In an I-Thou relationship, the Spirit is the third person. In the I-It relationship of selfish life, there is really no relationship as such at all. The object, which is frequently another person in this context, is used by the dominant subject without any acknowledgement of its integrity. It exists only to serve the subject. But when it is accepted as something of eternal meaning in its own right, the subject cherishes it and brings it to himself. And then the Holy Spirit, the third person of the Holy Trinity, infuses both with new life, so that each moves beyond the ephemeral to the eternal.

In a therapeutic relationship between analyst and analysand, the same truth holds. It is well-recognised that the healing wrought by the analytic process is not so much the bringing to light of hidden damaging memories from the unconscious as the creative relationship between the two persons. The analyst frequently substitutes for a parent figure who, perhaps for the first time in the analysand's life, is able to give love and recognition to him. As I have already emphasised, a mere intellectual understanding of the part past difficulties in relationships have played in our present malaise, does not in itself necessarily dispel that malaise and bring us to greater integration. It is the inscrutable work of the Spirit of God, Who binds up that which is broken, that leads us to a new understanding of the importance of past experiences in our growth to full humanity.

This Spirit works best in human relationships. Even Jesus was baptised by John the Baptist when the Spirit descended fully on Him, and He took His three closest disciples with Him both to the Mount of Transfiguration and the Garden of Gethsemane. On neither occasion did they show the slightest understanding of what they were witnessing — indeed during the Agony in the Garden they were asleep to the reality of the unfolding drama — but their presence must have strengthened Jesus for the trials to come. When the Spirit comes to us in solitude, even then we may be less alone than we believe. Surely the Communion of Saints is always available to us if we are available to God. This is an important aspect of the work of the Holy Spirit that we will have to consider later.

The healing Spirit never remains stationary. He impels us

onwards to the fulfilment of what we came in to attain. This is to become as perfect in ourselves as we see manifest in the person of Christ. In other words, healing is not concerned merely with the removal of a present illness or aberration, or even with making us more adapted to our present situation by infusing us with greater peace and forbearance. All this is certainly important, but in itself it does not lead us onward into the hidden country of santification. The Holy Spirit is that divine discontent that drives all creative persons on to their full stature as sons of God. He will allow the artist to be content with nothing less than a masterpiece that mirrors its divine source in an earthly medium, be it in the music, shape, or word. In the throes of his work, the scientist will sacrifice comfort and ease in order to penetrate the deepest secrets of the world in the service of truth. But the greatest masterpiece within human range is the perfect life. What great art presages is made real in the full life of man, the life indeed of a full man. No wonder St Irenaeus could say that "the glory of God is a living man," a man grown in the stature of Christ. Anyone who has received a mark of healing from the Spirit, whether this mark be physical, mental or emotional, is now obliged to lead a new life. This is the price paid for truly spiritual healing.

If the payment is not forthcoming, the mark of healing is withdrawn, and "the evil spirit returns with seven others to possess a psyche cleaned and ready to receive them." This statement applies not only to healing that has been given charismatically or sacramentally, and therefore has a "spiritual" aura about it. It applies equally to the healing of disease by medical or psychotherapeutic means. From this we gain the important insight that the failure of health which caused us to learn about the deepest realities of life is the beginning of true salvation. What a paradox it is that our failure of normal health is the beginning of real inner healing! Disease is potentially the Spirit's first agency of healing, in that it takes us beyond restricted, selfish ways of thought, and brings us to the mountain of purification. Until, as a result of the illness or suffering, we have glimpsed something of the truth about ourselves, especially the motives that dominate our lives and the selfishness that has been the central theme of our existence, we are in no position to receive full healing.

Jesus said to the man who had been crippled for thirty-eight years, "Do you want to recover?" (John 5: 1-15). This seems a strange question; surely the man who waited to be immersed in the healing waters of the Pool whose name was Bethesda desired healing above all else. Yet Jesus with His profound psychic sensitivity and psychological understanding knew that there was a deep fear of the consequences of health in this man despite his sincere longing to be made well. This is the human dilemma. The present state of things is what we really want because it makes no great demands on us. Indeed, a state of persistent ill health is an insidious excuse for an attitude of passive resignation to the difficulties of life. We can retreat into inadequacy instead of facing the challenge of constantly changing circumstances around us. Let me say at once that this cringing approach to the demands of a full life is nearly always unconscious. If only it could be brought into the open, we would be able to deal with it much more effectively. To attain health necessitates moving from an attitude of passive subservience to outer events and a dependence on other people to a condition of active, willed response to the world's demands. As I have already noted, the Holy Spirit moves us onwards. When He is involved, He does not relinquish us unless we relinquish Him, in which case He leaves us at the mercy of every possible difficulty and derangement. This is one reason why it is a terrible thing to fall into the hands of the living God (Hebrews 10:31). The cripple's life was certainly changed by his encounter with Jesus; not only was his physical defect cured, but he was also brought face to face with the challenge of religious orthodoxy. Furthermore — and most important of all — there was Jesus' later injunction, "Leave off your sinful ways, or you may suffer something worse." In other words, the thoughtless, selfish way of life that this man led, in common with his fellows, was no longer enough. He had now to show the power of the Spirit in his own life by becoming an agent of love and healing.

It is not surprising that most people practising what they dubiously call "spiritual healing" restrict themselves to a particular aspect of healing practice and look merely for an amelioration of some symptom. Seldom do they concern themselves with the full person. If they did, they would have to reflect rather more soberly on the course of their own lives than they were normally accustomed to do. This would reveal their own inner disorder, and few would be prepared to face it, let alone do something about it. It is much easier and far more agreeable to proffer healing to others than to have the humility to seek healing for oneself. "Physician, heal thyself" is the challenge of all who aspire to the spiritual life. If we can face our unhealed state with honesty and courage, we can, through that very incompleteness within us, act as remarkable instruments of God's grace. Our very lack of wholeness, once acknowledged, can bring us close to others, and by giving them something that we can ill afford, both they and we can grow in spiritual stature.

The widow's mite may well have contributed more to the coming of the Kingdom of God than the large sums of the rich and socially eligible people who frequented the Temple in Jerusalem. The Spirit works, as I have already noted, through people. But the people who are most filled with that Spirit are those who are emptiest of self-opinionation and arrogance, even the arrogance for God that is a feature of some types of dogmatic religion.

7

The Spirit and the Psyche

Do not trust any and every spirit, my friends; test the spirits, to see whether they are from God, for among those who have gone out into the world there are many prophets falsely inspired. This is how we may recognise the Spirit of God; every spirit which acknowledges that Jesus Christ has come in the flesh is from God, and every spirit which does not thus acknowledge Jesus is not from God. (1 John 4: 1-3)

IF THE PSYCHE can be equated with the mind of an individual, the psychic field of mankind is the collective shared consciousness of the entire human race. Carl Jung speaks of a "collective unconscious" that unites our primitive ancestors' thoughts, fears and aspirations with our own in a system of symbols and mythology. One thing is certain through our experience in relationships: we are not in psychic isolation. There is, as it were, an osmosis of feelings and thoughts between ourselves and others. In truth, "no man is an island, entire of itself." The outer material dependence we have one of another is merely a superficial expression of the deep inner coinherence that is the fundamental connexion between all living forms. The power that binds disparate forms, bringing them into a coherent pyschic whole, is the Spirit of God. He is the cement of all relationships. If He is excluded by a selfish action, that person excludes himself from psychic communion with his brothers.

Jesus tells us to come to terms promptly with anyone who

bears a grievance against us, lest we end up in a prison from which there is no release until we have paid up all we possess (Matthew 5: 25-26). This prison, seen in ultimate terms, is a state of isolation from our fellow men. If I have cheated or defrauded even one person, I have broken relationship with the whole human race, so tightly knit is our psychic solidarity. That person will have nothing to do with me, and I, in my turn, know that I have betrayed myself as well as the family from which I am derived. Until I put myself into alignment with the flow of psychic life once more by confessing my sin and seeking forgiveness (which, as I have already pointed out, is granted as soon as it is earnestly requested), I am inevitably separated from full fellowship with my brethren. The life of a criminal sees this psychic disintegration proceed to the point at which there is no effective communication between that person and the remainder of the world. No one trusts him or wants to know him. He becomes the foulest thing in the world. This is the real punishment of all who lead criminal lives or betray deep relationships with reckless abandon. By contrast, the penal systems that society has devised to deal with their criminal element constitute merely a mild deterrent.

It is also worth remembering that there is One alone who can redeem that criminal who has broken all psychic links with his brethren, the One Who though divine by nature, took on Himself the full burden of humanity. And the humanity was not only the glorified humanity of the healer and miracle worker, but also the stinking humanity of the Man on the Cross Who took the attributes of the criminal upon Himself and was regarded as the foulest thing in creation. He could link up even with those beyond human relationship in the state of hell, and reclaim them from the prison of death, bringing them through purification to salvation.

We are, assuredly, members one of another. As John Donne wrote in his *Devotions*: "Any man's death diminishes me, because I am involved in Mankind, therefore never send to know for whom the bell tolls, it tolls for thee." The medium of membership in the corporate unity of life is the psychic field. By it we know each other's disposition by sharing in it. We are in fellowship with the hopes and fears, the debasements and aspirations of all men by experiencing them in our own lives. It is in this sense that we can understand how Jesus took on Himself the psychic darkness of the entire human race when He was nailed to the Cross. Although He could not have experienced the sophisticated cruelties perpetrated by contemporary intelligence nor died of the terrible diseases to which we are all heir, He could and did experience the inner sickening, the dark loss of faith, the personal dread, and the uncommunicable loneliness that confronts each one of us as he contemplates the last moment of his mortal existence, whether in a concentration camp, an aeroplane accident, an earthquake, or by the terrible inroads of cancer. It is this irrevocable impotence that marks the end of mortal man. It is this shared knowledge of mortality that unites us psychically. Until that psychic medium which is the repository of all the hopes and fears of the human race since the beginning of its history is enlightened by the Spirit of God, it is a foul, airless enclosure. It is indeed the Sheol of Old Testament belief, where the shroud-like shades of the dead survive, moving in the noiseless tumult of agitated apathy. There purposeless motion prevails, and hope lies dormant in perpetual inertia. It is the Hades of Greek mythology, not a place of active suffering but of passive depersonalisation. Remember, even the agony of the Cross is not simply the physical pain of a tortured body, but the inroads of spiritual obscuration as the thought of God's rejection or even God's possible non-existence, suddenly impinges on the mind of the Anointed One. He took this on Himself so that even the knowledge of His divine origin (and by inheritance our divine spark also) might be occluded, at least temporarily, from His own sight. Then He could be identified with Hell, and in that union with the state of preternatural darkness, He could effect relationship with those souls incarcerated in its limitless dimensions by their own fault and through the sin of the world into which they had been conceived. As He gave of His

apparent worthlessness to those multitudes who had lived
worthless lives on earth, so His humiliation took on the
quality of glory, a glory revealed as uncreated light. This is
the light which enlightens every man, and made fully real as
it came into the world at the time of His ministry. It could at
last illuminate the dark recesses of Hell, proclaiming the
eternal victory of light over darkness, of life over death. It was
in this way that the realm of psychic fellowship was raised
from a dark, blurred underworld of wraith-like forms and
insubstantial apparitions to the full communion of glorified
souls working out their salvation in hope through the power
of the Holy Spirit.

St Paul says: "Be humble always and gentle, and patient
too. Be forbearing with one another and charitable. Spare no
effort to make fast with bonds of peace the unity which the
Spirit gives. There is one body and one Spirit, as there is also
one hope held out in God's call to you; one Lord, one faith,
one baptism; one God and Father of all, Who is over all and
through all and in all." (Ephesians 4: 2-6) It is the Spirit of
God that unites us, but we have to raise the pitch of that
unity to a living fellowship. When the Spirit is with us as a
conscious reality, mankind becomes a living organism. This is
the difference between a static, impersonal, cosmic harmony
and the dynamic flow of the whole created universe impelled
by the Spirit of God, a created universe "waiting in eager
expectation for God's sons to be revealed". This is the point of
concurrence of eternal life and the prophetic growth into the
knowledge of the Living God that is made manifest in the life
of a fully realised man, the life pre-eminently of Christ.

The entire cosmic life is mirrored in the psyche of a man.
There is a body, a soul, and a spirit. Thus man is carnal,
psychical, and spiritual. All three elements are of divine
origin, and none is to be exalted above the other. Man
mirrors the persons of the Holy Trinity; he is one being
comprising three elements that always act in close relationship but are distinct in themselves. The body acts, changing
the world around it, and by its suffering teaching the soul.
The soul informs and chastens the body until it is fit for

resurrection. The spirit leads the soul to its encounter with God, so that it may attain divinisation. But without the lowly, yet vibrant body of flesh and bones, this scheme of personal redemption could never be effected. The soul is rational, emotional, and possessed of will. It is personal and therefore tainted with selfishness. It is also the repository of the spirit within from which the Holy Spirit radiates. The transformation of the soul from a focus of self-centred consciousness to a God-centred source of benediction for the whole world is the end of man's life. The soul is the very centre of the personality, but until the Holy Spirit's effulgent brightness illuminates the soul, that person is in a state of darkness and imprisonment.

This is unfortunately the condition of most people today; they live at the level of self-centred gratification instead of divine realisation. In other words, they believe that the personal self-centred life is the authentic arbiter of truth, and they miss the deeper centre within, where the divine presence reigns. Man was created to be a god reflecting the nature of his Creator, and until he realises the Christhood within himself, he will find no inner peace. This insight helps us to evaluate psychical reality and understand how the psychic realm must be delivered from enslavement to the lower impulses by the sanctifying action of the Holy Spirit.

Many people have a degree of psychic awareness. They are able to effect a deep, non-rational relationship with the world around them and with people far removed from them in physical contact. Communication of a rational kind that uses sensory information is a very superficial manifestation of the deep inter-relatedness which is a natural property of all life. The Spirit of life, which is the eternal Creator Spirit, is the bond that relates all living forms and reminds them of their mutual dependence. If psychism could be seen as non-rational communication between separated forms of life, it would cease to have its eerie connotations of preternatural principalities and powers. The psychically sensitive person has the power of deep, silent communication with his fellows. In itself this is good, provided the communication is selfless and God-centred. And this is where the limitation of psychic contact lies; it is far too often a means of projecting the selfish ego on to others, rather than the way of loving fellowship in the power of the Holy Spirit.

Of all the creatures in this world, man most fully connects the body with the spirit through the soul. He functions as a person through psychic contact, and the effect of that contact lingers long after it has been made. Those of us who are sensitive remember a psychic impression because it impinges on us, and its savour is not easily dissipated. In the psychic dimension, memory has a timeless repository, and the souls of those who have died to the physical body survive and grow into full humanity. To be sure, their body is not an earthly one, since "flesh and blood can never possess the kingdom of God." (I Corinthians 15:50) The body is of spiritual substance, composed not of the corruptible matter of the earth, but of the attitudes of mind that have accrued from past experiences. These mental attitudes are the composite units of psychical reality. Some are beautiful and inspiring, and form the basis of a radiant spiritual body. Others are aberrant, broken and fit for nothing. They persist in the psychic dimension as a stumbling-block and try to attain completeness by possessing those which are radiant. As a soul dies to its body, so it finds its place according to the attitudes and values it once lived by. Thus the psychic world is a vast conglomeration of mental attitudes and emotional forces under the variable control of the will of those who function in that world. It is intrinsically no more evil than the physical world we all know, but because of its nebulous, intangible quality, it cannot be easily grasped, even by those who are psychically attuned. It is alternately a world of noble aspiration and dangerous delusion, and the more it is embraced, the more control does it assume and the greater the loss of personal free will does it exact from those who associate with it. But, as I have already noted, it is an integral part of reality, and no one can avoid contact with it, either at this present moment, or, even more significantly, after death. Were it not for our soul, where the authenticity of the personality is recognised, we would never make a relationship of meaning with anyone else. And this authenticity, whether it be of the saint or the criminal, is transmitted psychically from one person to another. It is the simple, the unencumbered, the gently receptive who attain psychic awareness. A small child can sometimes divine the unreliability of a grown-up person that an intellectually accomplished adult would entirely overlook. Indeed, one has to attain the openness of a little child before one can enter the kingdom of Heaven, which is probably a high state of psychic reality, at least in its introductory phase. Only with greater self-giving does the soul gain the vision of God, which is the One from Whom all love and light arise and bind the creation in a composite whole as undivided as the seamless robe of the crucified Christ.

Creation is indestructible. It is made by the Word of God, and it exists eternally in His Mind, the Mind of Christ. What we banish from the physical world persists in the psychic realms. Indeed, its psychic potency is enormously increased when it is deprived of a physical basis, since there is now nothing to contain it or limit it. This sobering thought is important when we consider the death of a wicked person or one who has been grievously wronged. If we think we have disposed of an unpleasant incubus from the realm of the living, we deceive ourselves. It is therefore contingent upon us to attempt the redemption of every living creature here on earth now, so that its aberrant psychic emanations may be annulled and eventually brought to cosmic harmony. Whenever we try to get our own revenge, we are adding to the cosmic disharmony of the world and ensuring our own discomfiture in the future. It is with these thoughts in mind that Jesus' great teaching about not setting ourselves against the man who wrongs us rings true. This does not mean ignoring the demand for justice; it means that gratuitous revenge must be eschewed. Justice administered is the first stage in the redemption of the wrong-doer. Revenge, on the other hand, assures that both he and we will remain outside the company of righteous men, as vindictive and unappeased as ever. Justice and compassion together can effect redemption, but the process may be a very long one.

The psychic field is therefore to be understood as the realm of habitation of insubstantial forms that emanate from the living and represent those who are no longer alive to the physical body. It is the means of communication on what may be called the soul, or truly personal level. It is promiscuous in its contacts, and is as unreliable morally as the world in which we live. All its inhabitants, which comprise what we collectively call "the living and the dead", are among the Communion of Saints, at least in potentiality. The true Communion of Saints has sworn its allegiance to God, and works selflessly to His service. These are the spirits that St John, in the passage from his first letter quoted at the beginning of this chapter, would describe as being from God. These spirits acknowledge that Jesus Christ has come in the flesh. I do not believe that a mere mental affirmation of the Incarnation of Jesus Christ is implied by this acknowledgement; presumably an evil spirit could make the same confession but without honest intent. What is required to prove the God-based authority of a spirit is the working of the Holy Spirit through it, so that it becomes a mouth-piece of God and the way of formulating truly prophetic teaching. To put this on a more earthly level, the person in contact with the Holy Spirit is inspired to come closer to Christ by being prepared to make a sacrifice of himself for others, whereas a falsely inspired person centres all demands on himself and grows in power at the expense of his fellows. He who leads the Christ-life is inspired by His Spirit. In other words, the "spirit of a good man made perfect", one who is in direct communion with the Spirit of God, leads us on our earthly plane of existence in the way of Christ. It leads us, through fellowship, to sacrifice our own interests for the coming of His kingdom. The end of our life is a realisation of the life He led when He was here in the flesh with us.

By contrast, an intermediate spirit in the psychic world inspires us falsely, so that we centre all life's demands on ourselves and attempt to attain personal power at the expense of others. The numerous subtle ideologies and cults around us at present emphasise this tendency for groups of individuals to grasp power for themselves under the guise of spiritual development. Those of us who become enslaved to the control of intermediate psychic presences are anchored to the world of illusion, where our own progress takes precedence over that of our brethren. In fact, as soon as we become restricted to ourselves, even in regard to spiritual progress, we at once move out of the light into the shadow realms of selfish craving. Those, I repeat, who are restricted to communication with the intermediary powers that inhabit the psychic world cannot see beyond that world. They place themselves at a distance from the knowledge of God's presence. The Holy Spirit, on the other hand, not only leads us to a full encounter with God the Father, but also attires us for the encounter. As we see Him, so we resemble Him. The image of God in which man was originally formed begins at last to radiate from the core of our personality.

I believe this Holy Spirit often comes to us through the medium of the Communion of Saints. These then effect the psychical transmission of God's message to us. The Communion of the "spirits of good men made perfect" takes us to the eternal source of power and love, where God's will is open to our knowledge.

If we are to experience the inspiration of the Holy Spirit, two demands must be met. Firstly our minds must be still; in silence alone can the Spirit be received. And secondly the psychic milieu must be cleansed and purified. There must be no intruding intermediary spirits liable to interfere with or diffuse the power of the Spirit.

It is in regard to this second requirement that the Communion of Saints is vitally important; it is the instrument of grace which allows the unimpeded descent of the Holy Spirit into the world of form and matter.

8

The Psychic Gifts of the Holy Spirit

There are varieties of gifts, but the same Spirit. There are varieties of service, but the same Lord. There are many forms of work, but all of them, in all men, are the work of the same God. In each of us, the Spirit is manifested in one particular way, for some useful purpose. (1 Corinthians 12:4-7)

THE GIFTS OF the Holy Spirit as enumerated in 1 Corinthians 12 are too familiar to require elaboration: wise speech, putting the deepest knowledge into words, faith, gifts of healing, miraculous powers, prophecy, distinguishing true spirits from false, ecstatic utterance of various kinds ("tongues"), and the ability to interpret it. St Paul emphasises that those composite gifts are the work of the one Holy Spirit and they are distributed separately to each individual at will. It seems to me that the basis of these gifts is a liberation of the person from the oppressive overseership of the rational mind so that the psychic faculty can be opened up and flow out in unrestrained relationship to those in its vicinity. The Spirit, Who, as we have already said, is the real agent of unity between people (and ultimately all the creatures of the universe) opens up the enclosed, fearful, intolerant ego so that a freer fellowship can be developed. And the mark of this freedom from restraint is an outpouring of psychic powers and the intensification of deep awareness between people and eventually between all creatures throughout the universe.

As we are liberated from the constricting power of the rational mind and all the inhibitions that have closed round us from our childhood onwards, so we become receptive on a deeper level of personality to the desires and attitudes of other people. We also begin to know ourselves better and can tolerate our dark, shadow side. This aspect of the work of the Holy Spirit I have touched on in a previous chapter, and I believe it is the primary manifestation of a truly spiritual development of a person. It leads him, through humiliation, to acceptance of himself as he now stands and thereby to an understanding of and compassion for other people also. This deeper awareness of the needs of others is the right path of psychic development, because its basis is concern for others rather than a desire for personal power over them. As psychic awareness develops, so the person becomes more deeply related to an increasing number of people, and also finds an augmented attunement to the full Communion of Saints. Eventually he knows these to be closer to himself than the people with whom he has social intercourse.

To many people the gifts of the Holy Spirit are accepted as manifestations of a direct contact between God and man. Personally, I think this is an over-simplification. The dispersion of many of these gifts among immature people and the bigotry of some who claim them does not match up to a divine collaboration. It is a spiritual law that those who are in direct communion with God become more Christ-like in their workaday lives. Jesus makes this very clear in his warning "Not everyone who calls me 'Lord' will enter the kingdom of Heaven, but only those who do the will of my heavenly Father." He goes on to say that even those who prophesy, cast out devils, and perform many miracles in His name will not be so much as recognised by Him. (Matthew 7: 21-23) And yet prophecy and miracle-working are among the gifts of the Holy Spirit, and there can be little doubt that exorcism is related to distinguishing the true spirits from false ones. It is evident that a person endowed with spiritual gifts may not be spiritually minded, but may use the gifts selfishly and unwisely. What distinguishes a truly spiritual person is his devotion to God which is made practical in his devotion to his fellow man. The criterion is again clear: "I tell you this: anything you did for one of my brothers here, however humble, you did for me." (Matthew 25:40) It is indeed the very humility of the action that proclaims its perfection; a grandiloquent gesture focuses attention on the agent and thereby sullies it.

Psychic powers are a natural endowment. We all possess them in some degree, but there is a class of people, called "sensitives", in whom these powers are well developed. The child is usually more psychically sensitive than the adult, probably because the rational, analytical aspect of its mind is still undeveloped; in addition, the personality is less rigid and well formed in childhood, and there is a greater ease of identification with the manifold forms of life. Enviable though this may be on a superficial level, it is essentially a stage on the way to full self-awareness, and as such it is necessary for this psychic attunement to wane as full self-awareness develops.

This point of view may disturb some people who believe, quite rightly, that liberation from the domination of the ego and identification with all life in the Holy Spirit is man's proper end. But it should be remembered that the ego, our point of absolute self-identification in the moment of action, is not only God-given, but is also the means by which we make an individual contribution to the scheme of things during our span of life on earth. In other words, while we are assuredly members one of another, that membership does not consist in shedding our individuality and fusing into a shapeless mass. It means giving of our particular essence, which is unique, freely and without reservation to the community, so that it is enriched by our special witness, while we, in turn, grow into a more complete person through the fellowship granted us by that community.

This distinction is of fundamental importance in the mystical life. We are to attain union with God as free agents, and not fusion, in which our essence is incorporated into the divine body, so that we lose our God-given identity in the process. Until our ego is fully developed, we cannot even know ourselves as persons in our own right, let alone assert our personality in our particular situation. If I am to function competently in life in a particular capacity, be it priest, doctor, artisan, or housewife, I must execute my work with authority, an authority that proceeds from my personal self (or ego). If I have no knowledge of or trust in that ego, I will have no confidence in my ability to perform that work, and as a result of this lack of identification with myself, I will not be able to play my proper role in the world's business. The object of the psychotherapeutic process is to enable the patient to come to a full knowledge of his ego, which, as I have previously indicated, may have been so submerged by early unhappy experiences that it has never had a chance to reveal itself. Then alone can he grow into the maturity of a full person.

The aim of the spiritual life is not the destruction of the ego but rather its fulfilment as the focus of identity that brings us to a knowledge of God. The ego has, in fact, to be transformed from an isolated point of self-awareness to the light within man from which the Holy Spirit radiates. "The first man, Adam, became an animate being (a living soul), whereas the last Adam has become a life-giving spirit." (I Corinthians 15:45) If the end of material man is to function as a self-directed person, the end of spiritual man is to be at one with God and through Him to raise up, from corruption, the whole created universe. It is only when the ego is well-formed and capable of choosing alternatives and judging situations, that its domination can be shed and it can be subservient to the power of the Holy Spirit. Before his ego has attained this degree of maturity and wisdom, it would be dangerous for the person to be in full psychic communication with the variable powers of this world and that of the life beyond death. They could easily overwhelm him and possess his consciousness.

This extreme state of affairs probably does occur in some instances of mental illness. That it does not occur in young children may be due to the close guardianship they enjoy from benevolent psychic forces. The presence of a "guardian angel", improbable as it may appear to the worldly-wise, has been confirmed in the lives of many people. If such a being exists, as I firmly believe to be the case from my own experience, it could protect the person from contact with undesirable psychic powers. But as the ego becomes more developed and the person functions as an independent unit, so he becomes less receptive to all psychic communication, whether beneficent or malign. This situation is seen to its most extreme degree in the destructive type of intellectual whose mental brilliance blinds him and cuts him off from all true fellowship.

From this we can understand that the spiritually aspiring person should have a well-grounded awareness of his own identity but should not be imprisoned in it. He should be so at ease in himself and joyful in his own being (without ceasing to be aware of his weaknesses and defects) that he can accept himself for what he is, and focus his attention outwards to other people and to God. It is far worthier to approach God in prayer with self-forgetful abandon and joy than to cringe before Him in abject self-abasement. The first attitude is one of true relationship, unworthy though we may know ourselves to be of this great honour; the second is really one of self-centred anxiety in which we are more concerned with ourselves than with God. It is unfortunate that much liturgical prayer stresses self-abasement to the exclusion of selfless love of God.

When the Holy Spirit is working authentically in a person his ego becomes strengthened, but at the same time he is able to flow out in greater concern to other people. It is this second feature that is related to the psychic function. In other words, a truly Spirit-filled person is in conscious psychic fellowship with the world, and is not simply the passive recipient of psychic emanations that are directed at him from all quarters. It therefore follows that he can begin to "test the spirits" as he would test an intellectual proposition, rationally and with an inner authority. It is this command of the psyche that marks the spiritually aspiring person. On the other hand, the psychic ingress into his own personality broadens his understanding of other people and brings him closer to God. Therefore neither the personal self nor the psychic power that proceeds from outside dominates the person. It is rather the Holy Spirit Who has this authority, informing the personal self and enabling it to test the spirits with a judgement that is both intellectual and intuitive.

When a person has attained this degree of command over his faculties, and paradoxically at the same time a freedom from the domination of his personal self, he is in a position to use with love and wisdom the gifts the Spirit provides. I have already noted that these psychic gifts are not necessarily supernaturally acquired. There are many people who are naturally endowed with such gifts, and these are as liable to cause harm as good. Which effect they have depends on the dedication and spiritual maturity of the person. A good example is the gift of "tongues", or ecstatic utterance in an unknown language. It is also called "glossolalia", and is often regarded as a direct manifestation of the inner baptism that the Holy Spirit confers. It is in effect a release of the emotional part of the psyche from the censorship of its rational component. Now at last the person can flow out in direct personal praise to God, Who, as the mystics have always known, is never comprehended by thought alone but only by a much deeper and freer giving of oneself. This is the secret of love, by which alone God may be known and held. The language of glossolalia is in many respects comparable to that used by an infant making its first verbal contact with its parents. When we remember that only those who can receive the kingdom of heaven as a little child can enter into it, we can grasp the precious nature of the inwardly directed prayer of praise. At once it opens the person to the needs and love of others, and it plays its part in bringing him into psychic communion with a body of believers and eventually with God Himself. In my opinion, if this gift is used properly, it leads the person into greater peace and silence, so that eventually the utterance may give way to contemplative union with God. When two people are first introduced to one another, they exchange much conversation, discovering the various outer attributes and interests they share. But as they grow into the harmony of love, they have less need of words and can spend hours together in silent union. This is the human counterpart to mystical prayer by which the soul contemplates God through the Spirit within it.

But this same gift in the possession of a spiritually immature person can easily become an object of exhibitionism. The one who has this gift uses it not only to praise God but also to impress his fellows. Soon an attitude of exclusiveness develops, so that those who have the gift feel themselves to be a people apart, a chosen group. The result of this is not the unity of the Holy Spirit but the divisiveness of the arrogant personal self governed by the lower impulses of self-aggrandisement and complacency. The gift of tongues can become a manifestation of hysteria in unbalanced people, who use it, quite unconsciously, to escape from the demands and difficulties of the world.

On the whole this gift is much more appropriate for private prayer than for public gatherings, except in a group of closely integrated people who love each other and have transcended the demands of personal recognition.

Another gift that is highly sought after and potentially very beneficial is that of healing. There are many natural healers, and again I believe that their gift is a psychic one. They are able to effect a close psychic link with the person in need and give something of themselves to that person. What the nature of this principle may be cannot be defined, in our present state of ignorance, on a scientific level, but the Holy Spirit, from Whom all life proceeds, is surely closely involved. There are some people in whose very company we feel better. There are some hospital visitors who radiate a sense of peace to all around them and can cleanse an emotionally charged atmosphere, bringing hope where before there was anxiety and darkness. Some such people have a healing touch. When they lay their hands on the body of someone who is ill, they effect a release from tension and pain. In some instances this effect proceeds to an improvement of an organic disease, sometimes to the extent of a remarkably rapid cure. Some healers of this type are quite unaware of their gift, being simple, practical people concerned with their everyday life to the exclusion of deeper, more metaphysical matters. And they are probably blessed in their mundane simplicity, for too deep an analysis of the problems of life can have a quenching effect on the flow of the Holy Spirit in one who is not yet ready for profound philosophical speculation.

Another class of natural healer, probably merely an extension of the one I have already described, claims contact with definite psychic entities, alternatively called "guides" or "spirits". And we would be ill advised to reject this testimony categorically. The intermediate psychic realm is inhabited, as I have already indicated, by the souls of both the living and the dead, all of whom have their own share in the Kingdom of God, even though many have separated themselves from a knowledge of that kingdom. The angelic hierarchy, again a subject of unbelief even to many Christians, is clearly involved in this realm. Angels are to be considered as messengers; their function is to carry the information of God the Holy Spirit to those limited in a physical body. They are of a different order to the "spirits" of people that inhabit the psychic realm. Their main attributes are power and light, and it is as such that they appear to receptive human beings. They have no form, but it is possible for the mind of the person who has perceived an angel to clothe it in mental imagery. As messengers they have no free will; in this respect they differ from human beings both in this world and in that beyond death. A good angel receives the message from the Holy Spirit, whereas a fallen angel is in bondage to the dark forces that dominate much of the material as well as the psychical world.

These statements are obviously terse and dogmatic, but, as Jesus told Nicodemus, "We speak of what we know, and testify to what we have seen." (John 3:11) They should be accepted according to the experience and insight of the reader. Those who cannot accept this account of the psychic realm should not reject it out of hand; I always advise sceptics to put indigestible concepts and ideas away in a mental drawer, perhaps for many years. And then a circumstance may arise in their own lives which may cause them to recall old, apparently outlandish teaching, and they can then review the stored concepts with a fresh mind.

Neither the "natural healer" nor the one attuned to intangible psychic forces need be directed by the Holy Spirit, although the Spirit can never be completely separated from human activity, since He is the life-giver. God makes the rain to fall on the just and unjust alike, and even Pilate could not have authorised the crucifixion of Jesus were he not in possession of God-given power. When the healing proceeds directly from the Holy Spirit, the healer finds himself detached from the domination of his ego and at one with the mind of Christ. In other words, the consciousness of the one who gives healing is far above the awareness of his own importance and the claims deriving from the personal self, and rests in perfect self-sacrifice before God. I would never suggest that such a healer by-passes the Communion of Saints and is in direct personal contact with God; I would reserve this claim only for the highest mystical experience in which there is an awareness of complete union with all things. But I would most sincerely assert that the Holy Spirit is in command, and that His communion with the one being healed is direct, and is unimpeded by either the personality of the healer or intermediate psychic forces.

If a psychic healer goes into a state of deep trance there can be little doubt that his ego has been submerged, but unfortunately his unguarded psyche is particularly vulnerable to the invasion of untested psychic forces, some of which might conceivably cause damage to him and his patients. It is for this reason that I distrust any state of deep dissociation from personal awareness. The Holy Spirit, on the other hand, invites our active co-operation whenever He works through us. At the same time He makes it clear to us that we are instruments of His healing power and not the agents of healing. Not even the most exalted psychic entities can claim to be agents of healing. This function belongs to the Holy

Spirit alone; all other aspects of the psyche are secondary factors.

The healing effected by the Holy Spirit is mystical in quality — by this I mean that it transfigures the person. Healing wrought by psychic or charismatic agencies (I personally believe they are essentially of the same nature, but this is a controversial matter which would be strongly denied by most people with pentecostal leanings) may indeed proceed from the Holy Spirit, but it is liable to be intercepted and even disturbed by intermediate psychic agencies and the unredeemed unconscious mind of the person who gives healing. The Communion of Saints can act against unwonted psychic intrusion from without, but it is only the progressive inner sanctification of the person who is a healing instrument that can prevent his own prejudices and aberrations interfering with the full flow of healing power from the Spirit of God. This is why I have stressed the consecration of the will and the regeneration of the personality in a previous section; until these objectives have been attained, at least to some considerable extent, any healing power that may proceed from that person is likely to be distorted and even perverted.

The healing gifts of the Spirit therefore have a natural, a psychical, and a divine component, and they all come from the one source, God the Holy Spirit. But whereas a natural healer may tend to take the credit for the results of his work and fall into the error of spiritual pride and exhibitionism, and a psychic healer may be completely dominated by psychic powers to whom he gives all authority, the healer who works under the power of God, revealed as a person in Christ, has escaped the imprisonment of self-centredness and the glamour of psychic triviality, and is one with eternal reality. Only when the Spirit is fully in command can the psychic powers work in harmony; likewise a healer filled with the Spirit experiences an integration of his personality and can function as a balanced person.

It is important to see how the healing gifts of the Spirit should be used in practice, how the will, consecrated by the Spirit, can work in partnership with the Spirit.

9

The Spirit in the World

Neither by force of arms nor by brute strength, but by my spirit! says the Lord of Hosts.(Zechariah 4:6)

THE HOLY SPIRIT enters fully into our lives when we are ready to receive Him. He does not overwhelm us so as to obliterate our own sense of identity; on the contrary, He inspires us to grow into something of the stature of a real person, potentially a son of God. Furthermore, that growth is not simply a transaction between God and the individual. The Communion of Saints is working in ceaseless collaboration for the sanctification of all life.

As I have already noted, this Communion consists not only of those in the greater world beyond death, but also of those aspiring to a knowledge of God on earth. Our growth into the stature of full persons is not an isolated process. We are to become members of the divine community of those dedicated to the good — indeed the Communion of Saints — both for our own fulfilment and for the unique contribution we make by our very essence to that community. I only begin to know what it is to be a real person when I have shed all selfish concerns, even for life itself, and have bequeathed all my attributes to the community out of deep love for its members. Individual growth without concern for the greater community merely separates me from my fellow creatures. But if I offer up myself, even to death, for God's Kingdom, I shall know true fellowship and I shall gain knowledge of the eternal principle within me.

This is a key teaching of the mystics of all religious traditions, and it is close to the heart of Jesus' gospel.

Jesus came into the world as a light for blind, struggling humanity. In man's association with the world, he had wandered far from the source of truth within him. Though fashioned in the image of God, he had been trapped in a slough of meaninglessness over the ages of his independent existence. He needed desperately to be brought back to the light of understanding. To bring this about, the Word of God spoke through many great teachers, who were entrusted with the thankless but ever joyous task of opening the eyes of those who were spiritually blind. These great souls were to release their brethren from the shackles of darkness and death, so that they might pass from darkness to light, from death to immortality.

It is hardly necessary for me to pay tribute to these servants of mankind by name. This is the realm of history and comparative religion. But a few great names stand out. The light that lightens every man enlightened the saints of India so that they were aware of the divinity and immortality inherent in all creatures. In the Buddha there was one who showed and taught the way of personal renunciation in right living, thinking and contemplating, so that the final impediment to divine realisation, the clamant, assertive ego, could be transcended and even annihilated. The Word spoke through the philosophers of Greece, through the brilliance of a liberated mind; in them intellectual speculation was united with mystical intuition to produce a synthesis that leads us to heaven described in the Enneads of Plotinus. In a different way the earthy prophets of Israel taught that God is known in the historical process and that righteousness in living is the great requirement for co-operating with Him.

It is noteworthy that, although the Word spoke through all these inspired agents, and His Spirit proceeded from them, they all had an individual light to shed on the human dilemma. None was more correct than the other; the aspect that the one might ignore because of his racial or historical background was the very teaching emphasised by the other. We are indeed all historically conditioned, as we all bear the scars and the glory of a particular racial and religious (or non-religious) background. The Buddha had no use for a personal god, whereas the religion of Israel was prophetic in inspiration; through its prophets God Himself spoke. In truth whatever is said about God is wrong, as Meister Eckhart declared. The Buddha, realising the harm personal assertions about God can do, and how God can easily be degraded to a man-like, an anthropomorphic image (a tendency only too obvious in early Old Testament religion) wisely discouraged his disciples from entering into futile speculations about the ultimate state of reality, but encouraged them instead to live the proper life and experience the Nirvanic state of self-transcendence. But such a religion can be cold and lack the glow of human relationships that comes from a full expression of the personal self. It also by-passes the historical process and pays far too little attention to the world in which we live. The genius of the religion of Israel acknowledged the world, its hatred as well as its love, and was, above all, an historical account of the personal God working in the lives of people. It is often not realised that the pre-exilic Jews had no clear-cut belief in the life beyond death. The great prophets could look forward to nothing more than a wraith-like existence in Sheol. While this may shock those of us who see the life of the world to come as an essential part of reality, and without which God's love to us would be of little worth, it is to the credit of those honest prophets that they taught the law of righteous-ness in terms of present actions in this world and not by promises of future punishments or rewards in an after-life. The people of Israel were gradually prepared for a wider appreciation of the survival of death through their contact with Babylonian, Persian, and Greek thought. On the other hand, the Hindu-Buddhist scheme has taken immortality as a basic principle of existence and on it has grafted a scheme of reincarnation. This again has a ring of truth about it, provided a return to this world is not insisted on as an invariable sequence, and of even greater importance, the round of rebirth is seen as one of growing into the knowledge and love of God. Where punishment and retribution are the main themes of an after-life state, the personal self is once more exalted to a dominant status in the life of the person.

In the life of Jesus, an unpretentious Palestinian Jew of the first century of our era, there was one who showed what it meant to be a full, proper human being. He was, like His predecessors, a great ethical teacher. In addition He had an understanding of the psychology of man that is a source of amazement to us even now. He was so attuned to the psychic dimension of reality that He could perform remarkable healing feats; even the natural world around Him was under His control. But, as I have stressed already and on more than one occasion, it was His perfect identification with His fellow-men that was His greatest achievement and His gift to us. To be sure, He revealed man at His most supreme, but He also came down to redeem those who were lost by becoming one with them and living through their agony until its last dread had been exposed and transformed into the radiant hope of eternal salvation. It was this renunciation of self in order to be able to take on the burden of the most debased criminal that marked Jesus out as distinct from any of His great predecessors. He is the image of eternal man, not simply by what He taught, or achieved, or even the life He lived, but by what He was in Himself when He took on the nature of failure, futility, and execration. Indeed, no man comes to the Father except by the way Jesus showed in His life. Of Him it can be said truly that He *is* the way, the truth and life itself. St John was inspired when he wrote: "He who possesses the Son has life indeed." (1 John 5:12)

It thus came about that in Jesus Christ, the Word of God not only speaks prophetically but also lives, suffers and dies with men. Only then is He resurrected to a glory even greater than was His before His incarnation. Most Christians believe that this supreme manifestation of God's Word in the world of form and change was also the final one. The canon of Holy Scripture ended, so it is asserted, with the last book of the

New Testament. After that the Spirit had nothing further of
theological importance to impart to mankind. But, alas, even
the Word made flesh Who dwells among us is soon misinter-
preted once He leaves us. His teaching tends to be misunderstood and even perverted. "The written word condemns to
death, but the Spirit gives life." (2 Corinthians 3:6) It is a
lamentable fact that once the new religion, Christianity, had
attained temporal power, it lapsed from its pristine love and
charity to become an instrument of persecution and destruction. It started to destroy the relics of Greek culture, and, had
it been allowed full dominion, it is conceivable that every
vestige of pre-Christian learning would have been lost to the
world. How apt is the prophecy of Zechariah quoted at the
beginning of the chapter!

And so it came about that God's Word spoke through the
Arabian prophet Mohammed. While few non-Moslems can
respond with enthusiasm to the violence of this very great
man and his successors, nor can they altogether accept his
teaching about the utter transcendence of God Whose power
is supreme and not to be questioned, there can be no doubt
that Islam was one of the great bastions of civilisation during
the dark ages of barbarism and Christian bigotry. While
darkness enveloped Northern and Central Europe, art,
science, and the wonderful mysticism of the Sufis illuminated
the world of Islam. Without the embracing liberalism of
many (but not all) Moslem rulers, there might have been no
continuity between Hellenistic thought and the modern
world of science and philosophy.

In this sequence of events we can clearly discern the Holy
Spirit at work in a prophet who lived six centuries after
Christ, who was inspired to found a new religion that was to
civilise vast areas of the world. Its complement of mystics and
saints testifies to its permanent importance in the world of
spiritual values. It has brought many different people to a
recognition of God's sovereignty in a world too often dominated by human power.

By the end of the Middle Ages, the Spirit of God was
working in many men. They had outgrown the limitation of

thought of their religious tradition, and were now ready to explore the tangible world of the senses with a new awareness of reality. The great discoveries of the natural scientists transformed mankind's view of the world. The Word of God in His creative manifestation and the Creator Spirit were becoming more available to man, at least at the level of his rational mind. The Spirit was directing him on to a fuller appreciation of the truth. This truth was primarily scientific, and man was enabled to penetrate to the very core of the inner mechanism of his environment. Today man is technically expert and of great intellectual understanding. He has been liberated from many of the shackles of past superstition. What he once attributed in terror to the power of God, he has now grasped, and often mastered, as a mere phenomenon of the natural world. Far from lamenting the advance in man's power, we should give thanks to God for it. Today intelligent people realise how intolerable it would be if the universe we inhabited could not be trusted for what it was. If God had a tendency to intervene in cosmic affairs when the mechanism He had devised broke down, not only would our lives be completely unpredictable, but, far worse, God would Himself be exposed as a faulty creator and sustainer of the universe.

"The law of the Lord is perfect and revives the soul," as Psalm Nineteen informs us. There is one law only, but it manifests itself physically, psychically, and spiritually according to our understanding of reality. It is indeed man's purpose to know this law, to co-operate with it, and to use it as co-heir with Christ in the resurrection of the world. As I have already noted, man's grasp of the physical laws that control his world is now very considerable. But the fully realised man, typified by Jesus, is in harmony with the higher psychical and spiritual dimensions of God's law also. This attunement with the law of God, and indeed His identification with that law, enabled Jesus to perform the signs and miracles described in the Gospel. The very concept of miracle implies a special intervention of God in the affairs of our world to achieve an effect outside the range of the natural order of things. As I have already stated, I do not believe God works in this way, but He enables the perfect man to do His works as He would have them done. This perfect man reveals in His life the divine image imprinted on the souls of all men, but left unmanifested in the lives of the great majority of mankind. What we see as a miracle is, I believe, a special gift from the Holy Spirit working through the Communion of Saints whereby energy of enormous potency is transmitted directly from the spiritual order of reality to the material, physical order of our world. The transference of rather less powerful psychical energy to this physical order is by now well authenticated in the lives of many people who have received what is called "spiritual healing", but what is more accurately psychic, or paranormal, healing from those who call themselves Spiritualists or Charismatics (as I have already indicated, I believe the basis of the healing power is the same in both instances, despite the antagonism each shares for the other's theological position). And I repeat, there is only one law, the law of God. The manifestation of this law in the physical energy that sustains the world is as divine as the psychical energy that emanates from the charismatic healer, or the spiritual radiance of the mystic and the saint.

The Word of God has never lacked a mouth-piece. He has spoken through the scientist, the philosopher and the artist as well as the theologian. His Spirit has inspired them to serve mankind with a burning dedication to the truth that cuts across all personal striving and advantage. The Spirit drives the creative person into the wilderness far from personal comfort, where he is rejected by the counsels of the worldly wise and exiled from the hollow conviviality of the conforming majority who desire to be left in peace to follow the well-tried routine of surface existence. The Spirit of God builds up, but He also casts down. What is no longer of service to the progress of mankind, what assumes the nature of a stumbling-block, is summarily demolished.

There is no sentimentality about the Spirit. An attitude that may have been perfectly appropriate at one stage in the history of mankind becomes outdated as the spiritual under-standing of humanity advances. The view of God that the ancient Hebrews had — a wrathful, jealous tribal potentate, who could be placated by animal sacrifices — became refined and universalised in the teachings of the later prophets. In Jesus, a God of love sufficient to be identified with the lowest man is finally revealed. God does not change, but man's view of Him is constantly shifting as he moves closer to the divine image engraved in his own soul.

The Word of God and the Spirit that proceeds from that Word have inflamed the hearts of many whose work it was to transcend limited, imprisoning views of reality. All too often a static, even reactionary aspect of religion has been the limiting factor in man's advance to freedom. The agent of limitation can easily be worshipped as the divine principle in aberrant forms of all the great religions. It is no wonder that atheism itself has, on occasion, been an instrument of divine grace. It was never the will of God that man should for ever remain a mere passenger, travelling to glory on the divine train. God willed man's freedom so that he could learn from the experience of life and make real the divinity inherent in him. The rather naïve intellectual atheism of past times may have truncated man's full nature, which is, among other attributes, inherently spiritual and intent on mastering the deepest mysteries of the universe, but it also threw man back on to his own resources. The astonishing advances in science of our own time have been based on a view of reality that sees man and nature as an end in their own right. This does not mean, of course, that many of the greatest scientists have not also been religious men, but simply that their intellectual perspectives were concentrated on achieving mastery of the world around them. Had their attention been dissipated in fascinating speculations about the meaning of the world they were investigating analytically, their contribution to knowledge would have been less, and they would not have been such profitable servants of mankind.

It has, therefore, also been necessary for the Holy Spirit to speak through other people about other aspects of reality. Man is more than simply an intellectual animal. He has a soul that seeks meaning in a dark, indifferent world, and a spirit that is at home only in the realm of eternal values. These modalities of human nature are not open to scientific investigation, at least by the methods of contemporary research. They are known by their existential impact on the life of the person, and by this I mean the effect that they have on our lives at the present moment in time. The Word has therefore not been silent in many contemporary movements that have emphasised a particular aspect of truth that has unfortunately been neglected by the great religious traditions of the world. These movements cannot be equated with the higher religions because they stress one aspect of truth to the virtual exclusion of the wider nature of reality. But their witness is important both in the positive message it brings and in the way that message shows its own inadequacy for the growth of the full man.

When atheistic materialism was at its height in the nineteenth century, the Spiritualistic movement was inaugurated. After making due allowance for hysteria, fraud, and superstition, there remains a body of evidence which clearly proves the existence of a psychic dimension of reality. It was to the credit to the practitioners of Spiritualism that a serious attempt was made to prove survival of death in order to provide comfort and reassurance for the bereaved. But it must be admitted that neither the intelligent agnostic nor the orthodox religious believer has been greatly moved from his previously held position by the claims of Spiritualism. This is because the movement has not succeeded in impressing either the scientist or the philosopher with its probity or the religious believer with its sanctity. What might have been an epoch-making advance in human understanding has passed unnoticed, if not derided, by most educated people. And yet some of the claims of Spiritualism are probably true, and if used with intelligence and reverence, it could shed much light on such articles of belief as the Resurrection of the Dead and the Communion of Saints. In fact the one positive benefit the Spiritualistic Movement has brought with it has been the establishment of a number of highly reputable societies devoted to the study of psychical phenomena. The reason

Spiritualism has foundered on the rocks of triviality and sensationalism is that its sights were raised only to the psychical level of reality and not to God Himself. Guidance from intermediate entities is never to be relied on, not only because of the mixed company of inhabitants of the psychic realm but also because even a well-intentioned entity is by no means infallible.

Anyone who looks for guidance outside his own centre will fall into serious error in the course of time. But even to have learned this painful lesson is no misfortune, and some people have graduated through the Spiritualistic Movement to a more mystical approach to reality.

Another movement that started in the nineteenth century was Christian Science. At a time when the Church's mission to heal the sick was ignored by almost all believers, the call to healing through mental identification with the perfection of God struck a chord in the lives of many chronically ill people. While the metaphysic on which Christian Science is based is clearly an inadequate account of the nature of reality, scarcely noticing such important factors as the holiness of matter, the redemptive value of suffering, and the uncomfortable fact of evil that transcends a mere error in the way it is thought about, the positive benefits of this system of thought should not be overlooked. It has emphasised the power of the mind over the body, and has been an unrecognised pioneer in what today is called psychosomatic medicine. As a man thinks, so indeed he becomes. The Buddha said this long ago in the very first sentence of the Dhammapada: "All that we are is the result of what we have thought; it is founded on our thoughts and made up of our thoughts." St Paul says in his very well-known exhortation from Philippians 4:8, "All that is true, ... noble, ... just, ... pure, ... lovable, ... gracious, whatever is excellent and admirable — fill your thoughts with these things." There is no doubt that the positive thinking of Christian Science can produce a calmness and evenness of temper that is very salutory in a world of stress and anxiety. But the truth lies deeper than Christian Science proclaims. It is what a man thinks in the unconscious part of his mind that especially influences his conduct and health.

The unconscious depths can be skated over by glib, superficial, edifying thoughts, but the ice is liable to crack and terrifying chasms be revealed. It is here that the deeper evil of the world lies hidden; it has to be exposed and redeemed, and not merely explained away as if it did not really exist. But when this deeper reality is acknowledged, the application of positive constructive thinking can be a valuable adjunct to the healing process. Where the system has failed is in not paying enough attention to the physical causes of disease or the state of sin common to us all, in the limitation of which we have to attain mastery over our lower nature with the help of the Holy Spirit. Once again a potentially valuable system of religious thought has proved inadequate because its methods are too circumscribed; it has emphasised healing of the body and mind through the power of thought, but has not given due attention to the social or psychological dimensions of human suffering and disorder.

A third noteworthy movement is modern Theosophy, founded in the latter part of the nineteenth century. It sought to rediscover in contemporary terms the ancient wisdom inherent in Hinduism, and as such has formed a valuable link between Eastern and Western religious thought. Its emphasis on meditation has played its part in the spiritual development of many people — once again a judgement on the inadequate provision much conventional religion has made for contemplative prayer and the study of mysticism amongst its adherents. In addition the Theosophical Movement has made a useful contribution to the mystery of human personality and its survival of physical death. But it too has failed to lead man to his full development in the image of God. This is due in part to its adulation of intermediate psychic personalities, who are called "Masters", to the comparative eclipse of the Godhead. This infatuation with the psychic realm is allied to a search for "occult" powers, which are invoked in meditation exercises. In this way divine grace is superseded by personal grasping. The result is that the human being strains after a god-like power without first attaining a Christ-like humility and self-sacrifice.

It therefore comes about that four contemporary ways of viewing the world — atheistic Humanism, Spiritualism, Christian Science (and related New Thought movements), and Theosophy — each have their contribution to make to the spiritual advance of man. Atheism develops man's own sense of responsibility so that he no longer relies in a supine way on a god-like father figure to do his thinking for him. Spiritualism broadens man's grasp of reality, bringing with it an introduction to the psychic dimension that is denied by atheistic materialism. Once this dimension is accepted, the immaterial principle, called mind and soul, is seen to extend beyond the limitation of matter, so that, even if mediumistic communication is dismissed, the possibility of survival of an aspect of the personality beyond physical death is no longer an unreasonable hypothesis. At once a number of the gifts of the Holy Spirit defined by St Paul in I Corinthians 12 fall into place — but not into the place of sanctity demanded by the truly spiritual person. Christian Science emphasises non-physical aspects of the healing process and exalts the evangelical virtue of faith — indeed faith in God's sustaining power and love. Theosophy stresses the intellectual and psychic unfoldment of man who could, if only he were functioning properly, be in full possession of many powers that are at present latent within him.

In my opinion none of these views of reality is adequate, because none can lead man to that mystical union with all things in which God Himself is known. This knowledge is not discursive or analytical. It is the knowledge of love whose nature it is to bring all creation together, unite with it, and so identify with it that we know as we are known, and work with Him as He works in us all. But these modern movements have the Spirit coursing through them. If their members were obedient to the Spirit of God, they would move beyond the confines of their various restraining systems of thought and explore new avenues of that Spirit. And in doing this they would at last be able to impart their particular insights to the body of rather staid, unimaginative religious believers, in whom the true orthodoxy still waits to live and transform the world. At the same time they would enlighten the hard, uninspired path of the unbeliever with hope and joy.

10

The Serving Spirit

The Spirit of the Lord God is upon me because the Lord has anointed me; he has sent me to bring good news to the humble, to bind up the broken-hearted, to proclaim liberty to captives and release to those in prison, to proclaim a year of the Lord's favour. (Isaiah 61: 1-2)

THE PROOF THAT the Holy Spirit is truly alive in a person lies in his changed attitude to the world. He is no longer centred in his own concerns, seeking his personal benefit. Nor does he feel the need to assert himself or even justify himself to others or to the world at large. Instead he knows an inner peace, a deeper repose, that is far removed from complacency.

This peace emanates from his own deep centre, where he is immutably fixed. From that centre, where the Spirit dwells in him, he can flow out in blessing to the world. Once you apprehend the truth within yourself, your approach to life is radically changed. You have been vouchsafed a security so strong that your balance can never be permanently disturbed. The attitude is described as "equanimity" or "holy indifference". In this state, the emotional response to outer events is calm and serene; success does not produce great elation nor does failure cast a shadow of depression. Each is seen to be a pageant in the passing show of life; this life persists long after the isolated events have faded into the recesses of the past.

The security of the Spirit within brings the well-known "fruits" with it; love, joy, peace, patience, kindness, goodness, fidelity, gentleness, and self-control (Galatians 5:22). The Spirit takes us beyond the fleeting pleasure of sensual delight and the evanescence of happiness that depends on favourable outer circumstances and an agreeable inner disposition to a state of constant inner radiance. This is the meaning of joy. It is the light that illuminates the whole personality from within the depths of the soul, where its nature is one with the Holy Spirit. This is the uncreated light by which God shows His outflowing energies to the mystically aware person. In the personality that light is transformed into an emotional radiance which illuminates the darkness and aimlessness of the world around it. This joy does not depend on sensual stimulation, equable surroundings, or even a warm temperament. Indeed, it persists even during moments of the greatest darkness when the world around you is falling into chaos. This is because the Spirit is not limited by material stability or even psychic sensitivity. We can then know intuitively that even if this world were to be destroyed, God would create new worlds, worlds that we may glimpse when we die.

The Spirit that emerges in us enables us to give unstinted service to the world. It is the freedom of this Spirit that makes us profitable servants. The Spirit liberates us from an undue reliance on results to justify our actions. Whatever arrests our emotional response so that we become attached to it, has the power to enslave us. It is only when we have passed beyond the need for personal reassurance and the comfort inherent in clinging to past associations that we can know true personal freedom. We can at last be ourselves without needing to possess things or people in order to substantiate our own identity, with the result that we can grant freedom to all those people whom previously we would have held in subjection. By doing this we can begin to rejoice as they attain their own authenticity. In this way we can glimpse that higher love of one for another, in which we hold the other in the deepest concern while at the same time leaving him unimpeded by emotional demands to work out his own life in a world of tumult and trial. Likewise, the affairs of our lives are presided over best when they are allowed their own impetus, which is a function of the Holy Spirit, and are not being constantly stirred on by our selfish solicitude. We do not realise how much our own obsessional intensity of purpose and thrusting zeal for what we regard as right principles hinder the progress of those very causes we hold most dear. How often does a personal desire for results from our actions, praiseworthy though these may be, exclude the Holy Spirit from the field of activity! His conscious presence is shut out, and everything for which we have toiled is rendered vain.

The advocates of many modern social, philanthropic, and spiritual movements (including the three I have already touched upon) injure their particular cause by this obsessional demand for results. Though these people are well intentioned and capable of great self-sacrifice, they live for results that will confirm their particular creed and crown their efforts. They yearn for personal approval and exaltation, nearly always without being consciously aware of this craving. People of this type are seriously incomplete in themselves, and need the substantiation that comes from an ideological triumph to attain a more stable balance and a firmer sense of identity.

Unfortunately this same criticism can be levelled at the missionary zeal and intolerant fervour of many of the adherents of the higher religions. They too are strengthened in their personality as well as their belief according to the number of people they can claim as converts. Religions that have a strongly dogmatic basis tend to attract those who are unsure of their own identity and need some outer formula of certainty to gain inner assurance. At present there are a considerable number of bizarre cults derived perversely from the higher religions. Their adherents claim to have absolute truth, so that any who will not accept their particular way to salvation are believed to be irrevocably doomed to hell, if not total extinction. The demands made on these disciples are hard and exacting; an outsider might wonder how anybody could be attracted to such an irrational system of belief and gain so paltry a material benefit from it. Indeed, many of these disciples are literally enslaved to the organisers of their particular cult. But they in their turn enjoy absolute certainty of salvation, so much so that their lives are controlled from without and they need no longer strive for enlightenment, or experience the pains inherent in spiritual growth. The one Person Who is excluded from their lives is the Holy Spirit.

Rigid systems of dogmatic belief substitute a heavy burden of imposed authority, whose claims it is forbidden to question, for the life-giving power of the Holy Spirit, who leads us into all truth as we are able to bear it. Indeed, "the written law condemns to death, but the Spirit gives life." This condemnation, which is total in many contemporary, irrational cults, is also at least partly true of some of those enthusiasts who have propagated the higher religions founded by the great saints of the world. It is important to consider the harm these people do to the causes they champion.

The saint sacrifices every material comfort, every worldly security, every good opinion that others might have had of him, so that he can venture forth into the wilderness, there to encounter truth. He will bring this truth back to his fellows and, perhaps to the sacrifice of his own life, lead them out of the bondage of illusion into the freedom that the Spirit bestows. Those who follow the way of the Spirit lead dangerous lives. They learn early what most of us barely glimpse before we die, that nothing in this world can be trusted, neither people, nor institutions (including religious ones), nor teachings. Each is limited by the age and circumstances in which it finds itself. One alone is to be relied on, the Holy Spirit Who proceeds from God and is God. And this Spirit makes Himself known definitively within the depths of each person's soul. To know the Spirit within is the end of the spiritual life, and its way of attainment is by the consecration of the will and the descent downwards into the darkness of the psyche, both personal and collective. The saint has overcome material and psychic illusion, and is in communion with the Spirit within him, which is the apex of the personality. He who knows the Spirit knows that the life of Christ is the only free life; at last the Word can be affirmed in that person's life.

But those who come afterwards hope to acquire this unitive knowledge by attaching themselves to the saint and his teaching. They expect to attain perfection by a punctilious observance of the outer forms of religion, which in themselves can no doubt be helpful methods of achieving inner peace and dedication. But this is at the barest foothills of the Mountain of Transfiguration. Deep within, they know that this way does not lead to the Kingdom of God, but in order to assuage their unease, they seek to influence others. In this way their attention is diverted from the spiritual quest — the unitive knowledge of God — and focussed on such secondary matters of the organisation of an institution and the number of people they have been able to influence. Those who follow the Word without being servants of the Word tend to single out a particular doctrine of the full teaching and to emphasise it to their own advantage. It may be personal salvation, survival of death, spiritual healing, or the second coming of the Messiah (to which all the higher religions look forward, though He is given a different name according to the particular religious tradition). Eventually their gospel is largely restricted to this one facet of truth to the virtual exclusion of the larger concerns of humanity. In other words, many of those who devote themselves to propagating a particular religious view are really using other people to supply their own need for recognition and inner certainty. They cast themselves in all sincerity in the role of servants of mankind, but are intent on absolute spiritual power over others. The Spirit has been dethroned and the personal self, gorgeously attired in religious raiment, sits triumphant in their lives. Were the effect not so destructive, one might laugh outright at the naive, unconscious hypocrisy that punctuates so much misguided religious activity.

Is dogma therefore wrong? Should we live according to our inner feelings about the rightness of things and discard all teaching based on religious authority? If we did that, there would be such chaos that we would long very soon for some central direction in our lives. This, in its present state, would be forthcoming from the secular arm with its strongly atheistic tendency, or else from some dominant cult with a bizarre master figure at its head. Dogma rightly understood is a system of teaching that comes from a divine source and has been transmitted to man through the agency of great spiritual leaders. These have been directly attuned to the Word within them (that was also before the creation of the world) and have been inspired by the Holy Spirit to proclaim the word to mankind. In the higher religions of the world, we see a coherent system of doctrine that can lead man from his isolated animal inheritance to participation in the divine life. The proof of the excellence of a religious tradition lies in the witness of its saints, in the illumination of its mystics, in the perfection of its art, and in the precision of its work in the world. No person can be a scientist, artist, mystic, and philosopher all in one unless he is a universal genius of rare calibre — and even then there is bound to be some unevenness in his personality. But an authentic religious community can, and should, contain these types of humanity amongst its members. This is because a great religious system fosters the potentialities latent in all its members by working towards the full development of man in the divine image implanted within him. It has a profound view of the destiny of man and the nature of the good life. It is in mystical communion with the eternal values of truth, beauty, and goodness (or love). And, above all, it brings these values down to earth.

True dogma is the way of abundant life. It is all-embracing, or catholic, in sympathy. Nothing that pertains to the world is outside its scope or beneath its consideration. It has much to say about such matters as survival of death, personal salvation, spiritual healing, and the divine manifestation in the world of limitation, but it is never restricted to any of them, nor does it exalt one above the other.

What then is the true dogma? Is it Buddhist, Hindu, Islamic, Jewish, or Christian? The answer is, to the discomfiture of the bigot and the joy of the mystic, that all these great religious systems, properly understood and lived, contain the true dogma, despite their very different emphases and their individual approaches to life. Their saints and mystics have shown that each way leads to the communion of the self with God, however He may be understood in mental concepts and verbal imagery. Once again, "the written law condemns to death, but the Spirit gives life."

The way taught by Jesus in the Sermon on the Mount is a dogmatic approach to the God-centred life, as are also His parables and, above all, His own life and ministry. The same can be said of the Buddha's teaching about suffering and the way to end it, as enunciated in the Four Noble Truths which culminate in the Noble Eight-Fold Path. The prophetic teaching of Judaism, starting with the Mosaic Law, is another dogmatic approach to fullness of being. The same can be said of Koranic doctrine. Nor can the sublimity of the Upanishads and the Bhagavadgita be relegated to a lesser place in the pantheon of human wisdom and sanctity.

The teaching is there. What is necessary is the living of this teaching. The founders of the religions lived them, thereby making these ways of life available to their fellow human beings. The saints of these traditions followed the same path, proved its reliability, and, by their own witness and in the power of the Spirit, blazed new trails of glory for mankind to follow. What is even more significant is that these saints paid homage to the same values and began to transcend the limiting barriers of their particular tradition as they moved towards communion with God. They began to show in their lives what they had long known in their minds, that love alone matters, and only by it is evil overcome and God apprehended.

When this catholic scheme of salvation, or healing of the whole body of mankind, is compared with the limited outlook and objectives of modern movements that aspire to spiritual understanding, the difference is very obvious. The practitioners of these movements and cults emphasise one factor in their teaching. It may be meditation, psychic development, positive thinking, or charismatic gifts. None of these in themselves is unworthy; indeed, meditation is a necessary precursor for the practice of deep prayer, and charismatic gifts should be the natural outcome of a truly spiritual life. But these can become, all too easily, an end in themselves, and the person who is proficient feels that he has attained great spiritual heights and is decidedly superior to his fellow men. The truly spiritual person never feels superior to anyone else; on the contrary, his love is such that he feels most closely identified with the outcasts of society, and his greatest desire is to be of some help to people from whom most of us would shrink in horror. As one progresses on the spiritual path, so one becomes increasingly aware of two truths; one's own insignificance and the amazing love of God. It is this love that transforms our insignificance into something of unique value for all men. When contemporary movements exploring spiritual reality can produce a literature of the same stature as that of the world's higher religions and when they are proclaimed by a company of saints comparable to those of the great religions, then will they have something of real value to show the world. At present they exist, as I have already pointed out, to emphasise a particular aspect of truth which has been inadequately acknowledged in the contemporary religious scene of a particular tradition.

Are then all the higher religions of the world of equal value? Are they all equally valid? The answer must be, and is emphasised by the pluralistic society in which we now live, that God, in His inscrutable wisdom, has determined that a number of different paths should be available for men to attain spiritual mastery and to know Him even as we are known by Him. This will naturally disconcert the religious bigot who demands that his way should alone be the right one. According to the principles of logic laid down by Aristotle on which the methods of science are based, only one of a number of contending propositions can be true. Therefore if, for example, Christian belief is true, it is inevitable that Buddhists and Moslems must be in error. However, the world of eternal values is not restricted by this very obliging, but extremely limited, view of truth. In the power of the Spirit, we are taken beyond the circumscribed logic of the sciences (a logic incidentally constantly challenged by the data of nuclear physics, and proved inadequate by them to explain the remarkable properties of the elementary particles which are the very stuff of what we call matter) to the logic of mysticism, in which any number of propositions have their own validity in a totality of truth whose nature is that of God.

In the divine society, as I have already mentioned, there is no loss of personal identity so that the individual becomes fused into a shapeless mass of humanity, such as occurs in the far from divine totalitarian state subservient to some political ideology, which is such a terrifying feature of our present time. There is, on the other hand, an intimate union, so that the individual ceases to be an isolated unit in an indifferent, unfriendly world, but becomes instead a member of a body of aspiring souls, in which his full personality can at last begin to flower. In this holy fellowship he ceases to be merely an isolated individual and starts to become a real person. His gifts, which are unique, contribute to the well-being of the whole community, which in turn calls forth those gifts by the recognition and love it accords that person. And this love does not depend on what the person has to offer the community, but simply on his vital presence within it, for, as St Paul says on more than one occasion, we are parts of the one body. This is the mystical body of the Word; it is potentially with us on earth, but will be fully revealed when the physical body is resurrected into all-embracing spiritual substance. In other words, the fusion of the individual into an amorphous mass denies the validity of the person and exalts the mass, which is subservient to an authoritarian external power. By contrast, mystical union exalts the person to a full status of deification, in that he realises his potentially divine stature in the divine community presided over by God, "in whom we live, and move, in whom we exist." In this community alone there is freedom to be oneself, to be the other, and to know God in oneself and in the other, and by His presence in and beyond all manifest things.

Following this line of thought, it becomes evident that each of the higher religions of the world has its own priceless gift to bestow. Without it the world would be immeasurably poorer. God, in His wisdom, has decreed by what we would call an accident of birth, that some should be born into one great tradition and others into another. Many nowadays are born into an environment of religious agnosticism, and this too is no tragedy when we consider some of the foul things that have been done in the name of religion. It could indeed be easier for the person of the future to come to his own religious understanding without too much conditioning in his child-hood, a conditioning that is as likely to alienate him from his ancestral faith as to draw him into it. The form of a religion is its dogmatic basis. If one is to progress on the spiritual path, one must accept the discipline laid down by the dogma. One will find the dogma, far from being the religion, is simply the outer way that leads one to the inner sanctuary. As Jesus said: "Whoever has the will to do the will of God shall know whether my teaching comes from Him or is merely my own." (John 7:17) This will has two components, a regard for the outer demands of religious observance and a punctilious concern for personal sanctity in terms of right relationship with the world. This consists in serving the world so that some of its burden and suffering may be relieved.

The latter of these components of true religion, a selfless concern for the world, will strike a ready chord in the hearts of most people, even if they themselves merely pay lip-service to this ideal. But why should religious observance be given equal emphasis? Surely it serves to divide people, and in addition is a waste of time which could better be spent in alleviating the world's tragedies! But without a life of prayer and inner discipline all our attempts at world service are certainly bound to fail. The religious dimension of our common life stresses our dependence on God and makes His Spirit more readily available to us. Even the most primitive races know this truth, but their aspiration is psychical rather than truly mystical, by which I mean an attainment of union with God Who is beyond limitation and is the ground of all being. The secular dimension of our common life teaches us that the grace of God comes not merely to redeem us personally, but to transform the world. And it is we who are the instruments of God's grace. If we aim at transforming the world by our own initiative, we will simply impose another system of dictatorship on our unhappy planet, which already bears the terrible scars of human insolence and pride. Nevertheless, it is the second component that is the vital one, for "faith, if it does not lead to action, is in itself a lifeless thing." (James 2:17) It is on the basis of the fruits of action that the world finally judges the claims of any religious faith. The fruits of spiritual action are described in the quotation from Isaiah which heads this chapter. They were spelled out even more definitively by Jesus at the beginning of His ministry (Luke 4:18), and they are of vital importance to the understanding of authentic spirituality, which is something distinct from religious observance, while at the same time closely connected with it.

We are called to bring hope to the humiliated, healing and sight to the broken and the blind, freedom to those who are enslaved, release to those imprisoned in the depths of their own mind, and to recall all men to God's unfailing love by showing Him to the world in our own lives. According to the urgency with which a religion transmits this summons in the lives of its believers, so it is judged in the world of eternal values. Its concern must be universal in sympathy so that no one is left outside the redemptive love of God. It must also free man from the illusion of dependence on any object, whether material or psychical, until his soul finds its eternal rest in God alone.

The eighteenth-century German man of letters and theologian, G.E. Lessing, was one of the pioneers of modern biblical criticism. He was also an early protagonist of religious tolerance and years ahead of his time in spiritual vision. He told the story of a father who bequeathed a precious ring to his favourite son. This ring had the power to bless the life of whomsoever wore it. But the father had two other sons also, and his love for them was so great that he could not bear to deprive them of a ring. And so he had two other rings fashioned which were identical in appearance to the original one. In due course he died, and it came about that each son inherited a similar ring, so that one could not be distinguished from another. There was great strife among the three young men as to who had acquired the genuine ring and who the counterfeit ones. And so they consulted a wise man to solve the problem. He too could not distinguish one ring from another. In the end he judged that the son who possessed the genuine ring would show its blessing in his life. Therefore he urged all the sons to live the life by which the ring he wore would be justified. Only by the quality of the life led would the ring be identified.

In this parable, Lessing symbolised the three great monotheistic religions: Judaism, Christianity, and Islam. We could add other religions also, but the lesson remains. In the end it is not the ring that blesses the wearer so much as the wearer who glorifies the ring. And let it not be assumed that the one who does possess the pearl of great price, which is in all of us though known by the few only, will lead the easiest or the most pleasant life. Judaism has known in its many tragic moments that God's chosen one suffers and serves according to the remarkable prophecy of Isaiah 53. Christians have seen the Incarnate Word typified in that same prophecy. The saints of all the great religions have born witness to it in their lives.

As Jesus said to the lawyer who questioned Him about the attainment of eternal life, after He had related the Parable of the Good Samaritan to him; "Go and do as he did." (Luke 10: 25-37) The claims of religious orthodoxy do not depend on the observance of the written word so much as the Spirit that proceeds from it.

11

The Spirit of Prayer

How lovely on the mountains are the feet of the herald who comes to proclaim prosperity and brings good news, the news of deliverance. (Isaiah 52:7)

THE SPIRIT SPEAKS through whomsoever He chooses. He does not inquire into the beliefs or ancestral background of the ones He selects, but He sees into a person's heart and knows whether the dedication to service is there.

The Word of God is a seed implanted in the soul of Everyman. It germinates at the moment of spiritual birth, so that Christ comes gradually to lead the person into the full exercise of his own unique gifts. It is an important observation that the Spirit acting authentically in a person's life, leads him on to a full encounter with the Christ, Who illuminates the apex of the soul. When the Spirit is allowed only a partial place in a person's life, His action is deflected and weakened by unconscious impulses and psychic debris in the environment. I believe the Spirit has been active in the lives of all those who have devoted themselves to the religious quest. But often He has been summarily dismissed when a certain level of reality has been attained. The Spirit is gentle but demanding. Like the wind it blows where it wills; you hear the sound of it, but you do not know where it comes from, or where it is going. (John 3:8) When the Spirit is not fully accepted in one's life, so that His transforming power cannot be properly realised, He goes elsewhere, leaving one unsatisfied and devoid of full guidance.

This is why the Holy Spirit is not the complete Godhead. Without the Creator Father and the emergent Word Who effects creation by an act of will, the work of the Spirit would have no power of direction. The Spirit's influence would soon become contaminated, weakened, and perverted by the ingress of intermediate psychic powers, and distorted by the conflicts that lie unresolved in hidden depths of the individual psyche. It is this interference with the purity of the Spirit's intention that has marred the various modern movements that have sought assiduously after spiritual truth. Even more tragically, the Spirit's work in the higher religions has often been vitiated and reversed by the lust for power, the intolerance and the demand for personal assurance that have so often characterised the lives of those who call themselves believers. The substance of St Paul's first letter to the Corinthians is a rebuke to an avowedly Christian community in receipt of the gifts of the Spirit which has nevertheless been deflected from the life of union with Christ by sectarian loyalties, immorality, lust, gluttony, and faltering belief. The Spirit is not a magician. He is God's gift to those who have opened themselves to the divine life. He will infuse us as we give of ourselves to God in worship and to our fellow men in service. As we become purer in intent and aspiration, so His brightness will illuminate us and cleanse us from inner impurities. But there will be no radiance or inner cleanliness if we do not play our part. Each great religious tradition has a way appointed by which mankind may be available to the Spirit's downflow.

This is the practice of prayer, without which we cannot hope to attain unitive knowledge of God. To be sure, God comes to us by grace, not we to Him by personal striving. Nevertheless, it is to the person who has given every thing he has in faith and love that the pearl of great price is revealed. Prayer is the acceptable way of effecting willed communication with God, because it is an act of self-giving and renunciation. It is the antithesis of grasping for spiritual things that is the method of the occultist who 'invokes' powers and qualities from the psychic world. The difference between prayer and occult meditation is so subtle that even, or perhaps I should rather say especially, highly intellectual people may fail to see the great divide that separates the two. In prayer a person gives of himself in humble adoration to God Who is beyond all names. By becoming nothing — as Jesus was on the Cross — he attains communion with that which too is nothing and is also the eternal Godhead. For God is assuredly No Thing, as the greatest mystics have taught the world.

Moses learnt this truth in the vision of the burning bush, while Jesus taught that God is a spirit, and those who worship Him must worship in spirit and in truth. (John 4:24) In occult meditation, the person, while acknowledging his inadequacy, strains after personal attributes that will raise his spiritual stature, so that he will become a better person. But the personal self is dominant and in charge of the spiritual development that is sought. Therefore God is brought down to the level of man instead of man being raised to union with God. The result of successful occult meditation is a dynamically powerful man who uses spiritual things for purely selfish motives, though often, in his blindness, he really believes he has the good of the world at heart. There is a very close bond between secular humanism and many schools of occultism that cultivate spiritual powers and even purport to believe in God.

True religion aims at spiritualising matter, not imprisoning God in it. The Incarnation is God's way of assuming material form in humility in order to raise matter from the corruption of decay to the eternal preservation of spiritual being. This is the distinctive glory of the Christian way and makes it, in my opinion, unique in showing mankind the process of deliverance. "Neither by force of arms, nor by brute strength, but by my Spirit" (Zechariah 4:6), speaks against the humanistic approach to deliverance from evil. But Christianity at its best could also add the reverse side of this truth: "Not by lifting myself above the world in meditation, nor by condemning its corruption, but by identifying myself with it in its deepest travail." This is the way of Jesus, the full Christ. But it must be said at once that the identification with the world's suffering that we are bidden to take upon ourselves is possible only when we are filled with the power of God's Spirit. And this is the outcome of contemplative prayer.

It is not without significance that the way of contemplation is far better charted in the Hindu-Buddhist tradition than in that of the Semitic, monotheistic religions. On the other hand, it is the prophetic religions of the West that have made the greatest contributions to social justice and scientific advancement. At present many intelligent Westerners are learning about the inner life of meditation from Eastern teachers. At the same time the Eastern nations are striving desperately to gain scientific and technicological expertise from the West, and have also imported from the Western world political systems that stress, at least in theory, social and economic justice. The danger is that the Eastern world may sacrifice its ageless wisdom on the altar of scientific and economic progress, while the younger people of the West, disillusioned by the tinsel of scientific positivism and the barrenness of humanistic materialism, may discard the dearly achieved intellectual integrity of their forefathers for irrational, pseudomystical cults and practices.

God, as Dame Julian of Norwich says, is the "ground of our beseeching", or as we would put it "the foundation of our prayer". St Paul reminds us that "we do not even know how we ought to pray, but through our inarticulate groans the Spirit Himself is pleading for us, and God Who searches our inmost being knows what the Spirit means, because He pleads for God's people in God's own way; and in everything, as we know, He co-operates for good with those who love God and are called according to His purpose." (Romans 8: 26-28) The meeting-place of prayer is the silence that comes from an acute awareness of our own inadequacy, or sinfulness (the failure to live up to our full humanity). When this load descends upon us, we are at last bereft of words, and in the silence the Spirit can speak to us of what He knows we most desperately lack. We can then, bereft of all pride and self-justification, speak to the Father directly through the Word Who is within us as well as eternally present in the Person of the Risen Lord, at least in terms of the Christian insight. In this way God speaks to God through us, and we are enabled to communicate directly with Him in the deepest concentration. The conversation may be an articulate verbal or mental confession and rejoicing, or it may be in tongues of ecstasy, or it may be in that wordless communion which is the deepest and most articulate of all relationships. The particular merit of this trinitarian approach is that God's transcendence is acknowledged, while at the same time He is recognised as the ground of the individual soul and also the spirit that proceeds from it. The indissoluble union between God and man is emphasised without making the error of identifying the two.

The result of the communion between God and man is the outpouring of the Spirit upon him, so that he becomes enlightened and sanctified. The Spirit is therefore both the foundation of our prayer and the end of it, an end that is no less than human sanctification. This sanctification is made manifest by the fruits of spiritual action as well as a transformed inner life (radiating the fruits of the Spirit of Galatians 5:22). The sanctified life is no longer limited by personal objectives and striving. The desires of the personal self — its need for comfort, recognition, and results — are transcended. The life of the saint can truly be called transpersonal — it has passed beyond personal demands to self-giving service in the world. And such a life is free; there is an escape from the bondage of the natural state of emotional attachment to other people's opinions and attitudes. At last one can serve without counting the cost, and love fully without keeping an inner account of deeds rendered and gratitude expressed by others. Love can never be real until it looks beyond the world of recognition and reward to the complete emancipation of all creation, so that it too may ascend to sanctification, and if sanctified, even to union with God.

Prayer is the inner response of the soul to God Who is known in contemplation. It has two components: the silent, solitary communion in the secret place of the Most High, which is the individual soul, and the shared worship in a community of beloved brethren. It is this aspect of prayer that each religious tradition has emphasised in its own particular way. The silent personal communion is taken for granted, but unfortunately too little instruction is afforded in it in many religious traditions. It is often assumed that the disciple can, by a simple act of will, enter into the depths of his own being and effect prayerful communion with God. This, alas, is far from easy except for those who are well on the way to mystical understanding — an understanding, I might add, that seems to be an inherent quality of the soul rather than something that is introduced by outside instruction or exhortation. In other words, the real inner prayer comes to those who are in conscious communication with the depths of their being, and can converse through these depths of soul substance with God Who is immanent as the Spirit.

Such effective inner prayer depends, I suggest, on three factors: firstly something that has been brought in with the person when he was conceived, secondly a discipline of meditation, and lastly assiduous work in the world in whatever capacity providence has seen fit to place that person. With regard to the first point, there is little doubt in my mind that some people come into the world with a remarkable inner balance and wisdom, while others, and even their siblings, may seem to be devoid of all deeper spirituality. These serene people have been called "old souls" by those who know, and the inference is that they have had previous experience of a life of limitation. Those who deny this possibility would explain their nature in terms of genetic constitution which enables them to have a favourable mental and emotional balance. It would be futile at this stage to debate the issue, and I personally believe that both factors must be given due weight of consideration. In any case, the real life of prayer can begin only at the moment of spiritual birth, which I have already described in an earlier section.

The discipline of prayer is learnt primarily by example from others on the way, and here a religious tradition is vitally important. To be sure, there are many at present who have acquired a particular technique of meditation or, more precisely, a technique of emptying the mind of discursive thought and charged emotion, and feel they have arrived at spiritual knowledge without the necessity of committing themselves to any religious teaching. But it does not require great insight to see the superficiality of this spirituality. It consists essentially of mental repose to which is added a feeling of complacency. In fact, some types of private meditation can have the effect of isolating the person not only from those around him, but also from his own centre.

The void where God is known is also a focus of loving warmth. .The void that private meditation may disclose in those without the basis of an authentic religious tradition is a diaphanous film that separates them from reality and isolates them in a fatuous world of private illusion. Eventually their spontaneity may be enveloped in a grey apathy that masks all genuine emotional responses and dulls the reasoning mind.

Meditation in a group of like-minded seekers is certainly an advance on this private, self-enclosed discipline. But the finest meditation is done in a full religious body in which all participants worship God — Who is mystery, for He is beyond any attribute one might envisage.

It is for this purpose that a liturgy and a sacramental life is a very important concomitant of prayer. Each religious tradition has its own approach to divine reality, and it takes the form of a communal service in which all present forget who they are or where they are going and instead give themselves fully to the moment in hand. The importance of a set liturgy is that it serves no earthly use. Therefore nothing personal is to be gained from it. Instead the mind is released for a period of time from material considerations, and can pause before the mystery of creation in awe in the fellowship of other believers. Of course, if a religious service is beautifully conducted, it ennobles the emotions aesthetically. Likewise, a fine address is intellectually inspiring, and if the

Holy Spirit is allowed to speak through the preacher, He may effect great changes in the attitudes of the members of the congregation. But in the end the work of worship, or the liturgy, is its own reward. The worshipper should be able to reach a state of inner peace through the discipline of withdrawal from the world for a period each week, or better still each day. If one attends a service of religious worship expecting something for oneself, one is very likely to depart unfilled. But if one enters in childlike simplicity of intent, one will leave in a state of peace and inner radiance. Some traditions have a liturgy of unexcelled beauty that lifts the worshipper to the very portals in heaven. This is admirable provided the worshipper descends to earth afterwards and resolves to bring heaven down to the world in which he lives. Other traditions worship in a stillness devoid of sensual content. This again is admirable provided the divinity inherent in the senses is not neglected and dismissed out of hand. Worship in stillness reminds us that God is a spirit, and we are closest to Him when we are arrayed in the whiteness of spiritual purity and the gold of aspiration.

Sacraments remind us of the holiness of matter: the waters of Baptism, the bread and the wine of common life glorified in the Eucharistic meal, the candle, the chalice. The food that we eat teaches us that God is present in every meal around a united table, where there is love among the members. In the Eucharist this love is augmented by the Real Presence of Christ, but even so the worshippers glorify the elements consecrated by the priest, as they all are glorified by the Risen Christ. And yet He is also present where even two or three are gathered together in His name. This name is not that of a particular sect or religion; the name of the universal, indwelling, yet transcendent Christ is love, a love for one's neighbour, who is every creature under heaven's rays. The common things of the world afford the most inspiring material for sacramental religion, for they are the stuff of the present moment.

Silence as the medium of prayer brings time to sacramental perfection; it raises up the present moment to timeless reality.

In this reality silence, hymns of praise, the things of this world, and fellowship one with another, whether here or in the life beyond death, are all united in the Body of Christ, which is the creative Word that is eternally making all things new. The Moslem who separates himself from the world on his mat and prays in the prescribed fashion five times a day is as close to God as the Jew who praises Him for the glory of perpetual creation, even in the actions and providence of that moment, or the Christian thanking Him for His inestimable love in the perpetual offering of the Word for man's redemption, commemorated sacramentally in the Eucharist. Buddhism too, which stresses contemplative absorption into the one great reality, described most perfectly as Nirvana in which all selfhood is annihilated, has its own use of material objects as a focus for inner stillness.

The end of prayer is union with God. He is known in the peace that passes all understanding, a peace in which time intersects with eternity, matter is refined into spirit as the body of the risen Christ, life is changed "in the twinkling of an eye" into immortality as death is swallowed up in victory. In God all contradictions coincide, for He is the resolution of every contradiction in a new synthesis. This is the immaculate conception from which all new inspiration proceeds. This is the virgin birth whereby the blessed parents conceive the divine child in chastity through the power of the Holy Spirit. The newly-born may be a philosophical thought, a flash of scientific intuition, the high inspiration of creative art, or the frail body of a child whose name is Jesus Christ, and Who is also one of us.

The more complete the religion, the more perfectly it balances the contemplative silence of eternity with a proper valuation of the stuff of this earth. To the sensualist it teaches the reality of the unseen world of eternity whose nature is Spirit. To the ascetic it shows the divinity of the common things of the world and the glory of everyday events. A complete religion awakens the vibrancy that is dormant in matter. It is the instrument by which the Spirit brings life to the world and leads men into truth, the truth inherent in the Word.

As I have said, each of the world's great religions has evolved a way of prayer, the end of which is communion of man with God, or absorption of the person into the ocean of limitless reality whose nature is being, awareness and bliss (to use a well-known Hindu description of the indescribable). I would not for one moment equate these two approaches to ultimate reality. Indeed, they appear, at least on the surface, to be diametrically opposed. But in mystical illumination they are found to complement each other, the one softening the unattractive features of the other. A strongly theistic religion tends to interpret God in the likeness of man, investing Him with the attributes of a superior human being, an anthropomorphic image in fact. A strongly non-theistic religion that sees ultimate reality in transpersonal terms only, ends up in an impersonality in which creatures lose their identity in the immensity of all-embracing reality. In such a religion the individual does not become a real person. Instead he merges with the void. I do not believe any creature was fashioned for this purpose. As I have already indicated, the personal self has to be transformed, not annihilated.

Religion is not simply a means to a transient union of man with God; this would be a limited objective, almost a spiritual luxury for a privileged class of human beings. The end of religion is the divinisation of man, so that he makes real, in his outer life, the divine image placed deeply within him. The Spirit performs this work by His indwelling radiance and His transcendent inspiration. These two views again appear to be radically opposed yet both contribute vital insights about the relationship of the Spirit to the world. Assuredly He is immanent in all created things; man is indeed able to be consciously aware of the Spirit working in him, so that he in turn can work in harmony with God. And yet the ordination hymn that opens, "Come, Holy Ghost, our souls inspire", is also profoundly true. The power of the Spirit descends on us as a dove from afar, as He did upon the apostles on the day of Pentecost, but admittedly also with tongues of fire.

In the mystical life, this paradox of transcendent immanence is resolved in the realisation that every creature is in psychic communion not only with his fellows but with the totality of creation and with God. The boundaries of the soul are so deep as to defy delineation, as Heraclitus once remarked. It is this coinherence of all things that is the secret of intercessory prayer. When a group, or even a single person, remembers with love a person in difficulty, the Spirit of Christ is among the intercessors, and communes with the one for whom prayers are offered. Love knows no limits, and the Holy Spirit is present in all places at once, since He works beyond temporal and spatial limitations. In this way He is available to all who will accept His service. But He does not force Himself on those who do not receive Him gladly, in the way that Jesus was heard by the common people. This quality of unobtrusive humility typifies the action of the Holy Spirit. It is also a vitally important guideline for our way, who are instruments of the Spirit, at work among our fellow-men. On the other hand, assiduous work in the world in loving service to others makes our prayer life real and brings it to fruition.

In the life of Jesus there seemed so much activity that it is remarkable He had any time for constructive thought or teaching. His secret was the ability to pass through the midst of people. These were not only the hostile crowds or even His supporters, from whom He escaped into the silence of a hidden place of retreat. He could enter the secret place of the Most High even when He was conversing with people, performing acts of healing, or addressing multitudes. He called in silence to the Father, and the Holy Spirit filled Him with peace. He did not need to prepare notes for His teaching. Indeed, He told His disciples that, when they were arraigned before the seats of authority and power because of their allegiance to Him, they should not prepare a defence beforehand; He Himself would give them power of utterance and a wisdom which no opponent would be able to resist or refute. (Luke 21: 12-15) It is this gift of being able to call on the Holy Spirit at all times that is the fruit of silent prayer.

The Spirit can guide one into truth provided one has the humility to wait upon Him in silence with a pure heart. It is our own emotional imbalance that prevents our prayers being fully answered, because we interpose our prejudices between our will and the Spirit of God. We claim, and even believe, that we want God's will to be done, but in fact we want Him to support our own opinions and enterprises. Until we attain the deep silence of trust, the promise of Jesus, "Ask, and you will receive; seek, and you will find; knock, and the door will be opened" (Matthew 7:7), will not be fulfilled. We have to ask, to seek, to knock — this is where we fail.

Asking means enquiring about the very nature of our present difficulty; seeking is no less than giving up everything we possess for the kingdom of God; knocking requires a complete change in attitude to life. If we are prepared to ask, to seek, and to knock in that spirit of dedication, the Spirit of God will come to us and open the door of reality.

12

Humility and the Spirit

Rejoice, rejoice, daughter of Zion, shout aloud, daughter of Jerusalem;
for see, your king is coming to you, his cause won, his victory gained,
humble and mounted on an ass, on a foal, the young of a she-ass.
(Zechariah 9:9)

HUMILITY IS NOT an assertion, or even a real conviction, of our
own intrinsic worthlessness in the scheme of things, nor is it a
belief in the unimportance of our own opinions. People who
put forward their views tentatively and with apparent
diffidence, stressing how inexpert they are in the matter
under discussion, are in fact exalting themselves in the eyes of
others. They wish to appear as paragons of modesty in order
to impress other people. Humility is often a pose adopted by
those who want to gain the attention of their fellows. This
attitude is an important pointer to a deep inner resentment
the person feels because of the neglect he believes is his lot,
but it has no spiritual value. No opinion should bear any
trace of self-abasement; if it is worth stating, it brings with it
a personal authority. And no person is to be dismissed as
trivial no matter how unattractive he may appear and of
what little account his views on life may seem to the world.
Humility must not, in other words, be equated with self-
effacement.

True humility is closer to self-forgetfulness. The really
humble person is unaware of his own importance — or lack of

it — in the wider issues of life. A humble person is receptive, and is always capable of learning something new. His mentor is life itself, and his instructors are those numerous other people, usually dull and unprepossessing, who crowd in on him day by day. The antithesis of humility is therefore not so much self-exaltation as pride. Pride so closes a person in on himself that he cannot receive anything from another source. The basis of pride is, unfortunately, in the great majority of instances, an undervaluation of the individual by the society, including his parents, which nurtured him. Having no real faith in his own worth, he becomes so vulnerable to the casual assaults of the world that he shuts himself off from painful social intercourse by fashioning a hard, barely penetrable shell around himself. Until this facade of self-sufficiency is demolished by a calamity so great that it forces him to seek succour from the outside world, he lives in a private realm of lonely self-regard, secure in the knowledge that he is the possessor of the real truth and needs no one else to support him. In this way he is spared the wounding challenge of any new relationship. Only the proverbial fall can start the process of regeneration in a proud person's soul.

The fruits of pride are insensitivity to others, arrogance, self-righteousness, and an inability to receive love. Whatever goodwill is shown to a proud person is dismissed as patronage. There can be no growth where pride dominates — whether the growth is of the mind or the soul. Pride is a morass which holds the individual in a fixed attitude of mind and prevents him joining his fellows in the greater affairs of life. Pride, in fact, invalidates, indeed prevents, any effective personal relationship. A proud person cannot tolerate the possibility of his being mistaken. It is essential for his mental stability that he be always proved in the right. Proud people often afflict the courts of religion and the temples of worship, while pride is often the predominant attitude of those who aspire to spiritual knowledge.

Many people who are undoubtedly gifted intellectually or psychically are dominated by pride. Even considerable gifts of healing are often thwarted because their possessor, forgetting he is merely an instrument of God's grace, lacks the humility to learn from those with a different approach to life from his own, and especially from those who come to him for counsel or for healing. The Holy Spirit makes His home in the humble soul who can receive Him in dedicated service. In turn He sanctifies the natural gifts entrusted to that person. The Spirit cannot enter the locked heart of a proud man. "Here I stand knocking at the door; if anyone hears my voice and opens the door, I will come and sit down to supper with him and he with me." (Revelation 3:20) It needs to be said that this knocking is not only from outside the person's consciousness, but also from within the soul where the Spirit dwells in silence. The proud man is too full of his own riches to have room in the inn of his own soul for the Spirit of God. In the words of the Magnificat: "The hungry he has satisfied with good things, the rich sent empty away." (Luke 1:53)

It is not the riches themselves — whether material, intellectual, or psychical — that are harmful, but the attitude of exclusiveness, or pride, that they can engender in those who believe they possess them. The law is that "you received without cost; give without charge." (Matthew 10:8) As we give, so we are replenished and enriched. Those empty of self-regard are full of the Spirit of God, while those who use their talents with enterprise gain a double portion of their value. Those who bury their talents are diminished, for they have not taken the opportunity God offered them to grow in stature both by the experience of life and by fruitful relationships with other people. It is also possible to use one's talents in a self-centred way, so as to enslave those whom one attempts to counsel or to heal. This is where pride is augmented by the sin of arrogance, and it is a constant hazard of all those engaged in spiritual, religious, and healing works.

The person who acts arrogantly is usually blissfully un-aware of his deeper motives, and is earnestly intent on saving people from their sins or their ignorance (the two often merge). This defect is one of insensitivity to others and disregard for their opinions and way of life, which he seldom has the courtesy, let alone the patience, to investigate. He cannot, in other words, relate properly to other people, and treats them simply as objects on which to expend his charity rather in the same way as a certain type of idealistic theorist treats humanity in his well-meaning, but overbearing social or educational experimentation. There is an arrogant disregard for the finer feelings of other people, which results from a proud, cold, self-enclosed consciousness, and all who conflict with this self-enclosure or threaten its security are treated as fools or scoundrels.

This fundamental error in social relationships is an ever-present hazard in the lives of all those who are devoted to a particular system of thought, be it atheistic or deeply religious. In the case of an atheistic humanist, his view of life allows for no principle outside human reason, therefore all progress depends on the skill and ingenuity of the mind. It is inevitable, with this view, that those who are the best developed technically and intellectually should govern the lives of those who are apparently less gifted in these respects — or more probably less assertive and articulate. The end-result is a dictatorship. The trends in those political systems that have dispensed with God are now sufficiently well known — they do not attract those of us who value personal freedom. Man's insolent pride, which is called hubris, is the demonic element in the world, and its evil repercussions extend far beyond human society.

The same judgement is unfortunately true of the world's major religions. Each has on occasion been the agency of great tyranny. Their protagonists have restricted human thought and curtailed basic liberty in the name of God. No major denomination is free from this reproach. I have already described in a previous section the weakness in a certain type of religious devotee that makes him act in an authoritarian manner: a deep inner insecurity. Only a conviction that he is in possession of the whole truth can arrest the inroads of subtle doubt which, if allowed free rein, would undermine his belief in himself. It is assuredly good to know that even if things are not going well with one on a material level, one is at least secure spiritually and destined for great things, if not now, at least when one dies.

This approach to religious truth has been parodied well by the Marxist, but the reply to this criticism has not even now been fully formulated by many Christians with a strong missionary zeal. Many theists have accepted the social criticism of Marxism by insisting on social and economic justice, which is surely all to the good. But the aim of religion is something more than the attainment of an earthly utopia. It is the transformation of humanity in the likeness of God — seen in Christian terms in the form of Jesus Christ. The one important insight that Marxist social criticism has to offer is that this transformation must begin at once, in the world in which we find ourselves, and not in some other place and condition in a problematical life after death. By this I do not imply any scepticism about survival of the essential part of the personality when the "outer man" finally perishes. I personally have had enough intimate experiences of the life beyond death not to be seriously disturbed by the possibility of complete annihilation of the individual when the physical body dies. And yet the further I progress on the spiritual path, the less concerned do I become about the state of the person in the life hereafter. The aim of the spiritual life is to prepare in each moment of present time for the full development of a real person, so that when death does finally occur, something of real worth may have been fashioned to continue an inevitable post-mortem existence. The inevitability of survival of death is a measure of God's love for His creatures; that which He has created He will not allow to perish. But what actually does survive death depends in no small measure on the life of the individual while on earth.

These two concepts are, I feel, vital for a real understanding of the meaning of life and the work of the Spirit of God in man's sanctification: the immortality of the soul and the resurrection of the body. The first is a Hellenistic insight, and comes into Hebrew thought fully in the apocryphal Book of Wisdom believed to have been written some 50 years before the Christian era. The second is Hebraic; when the Jews finally did come to a belief in survival of death, they could envisage this only in terms of a resurrection of the whole person, body and soul. This is stated categorically in the Book of Daniel (12:2) and in the apocryphal Second Book of Maccabees (7:9; 12: 38-45 and 14:46), both of which were probably written about 150 years before the Christian era. There is a tendency among orthodox Christians to disparage the Hellenistic view of immortality and to exalt the Hebraic insight about resurrection. On the other hand those with Spiritualistic, Theosophical, and Hindu-Buddhist beliefs have no use whatsoever for a bodily resurrection. On a crudely physical level, they are surely right. St Paul himself says that flesh and blood can never possess the kingdom of God. (1 Corinthians 15:50) On the other hand, the objection that many Christians have to the doctrine of the immortality of the soul is that it is too mechanical: it seems to imply that the soul automatically survives by virtue of its intrinsic merit. In this respect, the Christian objection is valid and worthy of deep consideration. The doctrine of the resurrection of the body would, it is said, place the gift of survival in God's hands: only those who were worthy would enjoy a resurrection, whereas the remainder would either perish finally or else be cast forever into the outer darkness where there is wailing and grinding of teeth — to use a symbolism loved by St Matthew in his Gospel.

Neither view of survival is, in my view, adequate on its own, yet each possesses profound insights that cannot be discarded. The soul's immortality seems to be, as I have already stated, an inevitable result of the love God has for His creatures. Assuredly it is not merited by the creature, but determined by the Creator. Love cannot envisage the total destruction of any finite being. God, who judges the heart, knows more than man ever can, the root of the evil in any person. What we call sin is usually a compound of environmental deprivation and individual inadequacy. In any instance, one of these two is bound to predominate, but in even the most evil person there is surely some spark of goodness, for God created him also. Therefore I look for the redemption of all creatures after much tribulation in an intermediate state of being. I derive this hope not so much from the Bible (which is equivocal on this matter) as from my knowledge of God's unfailing love.

But God's love is not indiscriminate or sentimental. It is stern and demanding. God will, speaking figuratively, not lift a finger to help someone who is on the downward moral path until he himself prays fervently for help. And this true prayer comes only at the depth of great suffering. Until the person has faced his own responsibilities with honesty and courage, he cannot know God's love, because he will not avail himself of it. Such a person can find, to his consternation, that he has survived death in a formless state. He has built no spiritual body from the good deeds and noble thoughts that should have been his while he was on earth. Such a person quite literally survives as an earth-bound wraith, if he is not surrounded by the impenetrable darkness of the lowest plane of the after-life, which we call hell. This is a dire punishment, but the one who inflicts it is the person himself by virtue of the destructive life he has led. God does not punish that person. Indeed, it is God's greatest desire that all who are lost should return home as the Prodigal Son did. But until the sinner comes to his senses, he will remain in spiritual isolation and darkness. I believe, however, that there is an opportunity for all discarnate personalities to repent even in the after-life, and then the blessed Communion of Saints can befriend them and initiate the process of redemption.

This full process will require much purification and learning in the life of the world to come, but there is always hope that, in the course of a time outside our time, this person, cleansed of all guilt by the love of God at last fully accepted, will be able to fashion a real spiritual body composed of noble thoughts, loving attitudes, and the fruit of unremitting service in other realms but always to finite beings. We are indeed being born anew each day. "Though our outward humanity is in decay, yet day by day we are inwardly renewed." (2 Corinthians 4:16) It does not seem to me to be unlikely that this process of renewal, or rebirth into a nobler frame and a higher consciousness, proceeds even after the physical body has been discarded. And in the end even the physical body that marks our time of humiliation as we grow decrepit and old is to be transfigured, resurrected, and brought into the eternal glory of spiritual essence. This is the far-off event to which the whole creation moves in stumbling steps, led by a little child whose name is Christ, the ever-renewing Word of God.

To sum up an intricate, but important matter: the soul's immortality is assured because God loves His creatures, and will not let any perish. This free grace is not dependent on the creature's character but on God's unfailing mercy. On the other hand, the body of spiritual substance that clothes the soul, gives it form, and sends it into the greater life beyond death, is a product of the life the person has led while he was alive in the flesh of this world. The quality of our spiritual body is determined by the quality of our thoughts, words, and actions now. We continue to build this body during every experience, every encounter, every sacrifice, every moment of our present life, which is also eternal life.

This being so, what is the duty of any religious person to his unawakened brethren? Should he be exhorting them to be converted to the truth, to God, to Christ, so that they may be saved from the wrath to come, both in this life and the life of the world to come? Or should he mind his own business and let the unbeliever get on with his own life? I feel that neither approach is wholly right. The first is arrogant and has as its motivating force fear and punishment. It not only gives a wrong account of the nature of God, equating Him with the wrathful potentiate of the early Old Testament rather than the Lord of love typified by Jesus, but it also lays too great a stress on individual salvation. It must be said directly that the person who lives according to rules and precepts, who affirms credal statements, and follows prescribed rituals in order to attain heavenly status is not leading the good life. The centre of his world is his unredeemed personal self striving desperately for immortality and making use of religion to attain this end. The situation is not so very different in its essence from that of the ambitious young person who does the right things and cultivates the right people with the unashamed purpose of getting on in the world. Religions that stress the urgency for personal salvation in these terms of reference do not lead to the fulfilment of a complete personality. They err also in seeing situations either in white or in black; the reconciliation that understanding and compassion introduce is foreign to their outlook. There is an arrogant disregard for other points of view, a static attitude to developing situations, and an inability to accommodate the inflow of the Holy Spirit. In other words, a rigid view of salvation, no matter how doctrinally based it is, limits the freedom of the human mind and fails in its purpose of healing the person.

The converse attitude, of leaving other people to their own spiritual devices and pursuing one's own religious path, is certainly less objectionable and shows greater respect for points of view other than one's own. But it has a certain coldness and detachment about it, for it lacks the warmth of true human relationship. If one believes one has really found something of supreme value in one's life, one's joy is such that one cannot help but impart the good news to others. The good news, or gospel, that Jesus came to proclaim was that the time had come; the Kingdom of God was upon the world. Now was the time for repentance, for a change in heart. (Mark 1:15) His ministry was directed to making that repentance possible and to showing what the kingdom of God meant in worldly living.

Jesus came, as St John saw so clearly, that men might have life, and have it in all its fullness. (10:10) Those of us who follow Him, or for that matter any other religious teacher, will be judged by the measure of fullness we show in our own lives and the fullness we bring to the lives of others. Exhortations, threats and claims do not impress those with intelligence and discernment. It is the fruit of spiritual living that makes the claims valid, and the fruit is a present change in the lives of people. As we lead our present lives, so the future is determined; this applies not only to this world but to the after-life also. The urgency of the Gospel (or any system of

religious doctrine) is not to save people from the wrath to
come, but to release them from the bondage of fear,
impotence, hatred and purposelessness that is their present
lot. They must be brought into a creative relationship with
their present circumstances. Hell is not primarily a realm
where people who have lived sinful lives find themselves
when they die. It is first and foremost a very present state of
desolation, of isolation, of perpetual, meaningless existence
that many of us are experiencing at this present moment. It is
the antithesis of the Kingdom of God that Jesus came to
proclaim. It will most certainly persist in the future and be
carried on in the life after death until there is a change in
heart of the person. Even those whose lives appear on the
surface to be enviable and outwardly successful are often, if
not to some extent always, in some inner difficulty, some
hidden distress, the victim of incipient fear and desolation.
Only the very foolish would equate outer prosperity with
inner peace. The first is a passing event, liable to be followed
at any time by misfortune and humiliation; the second is a
spiritual blessing that will persist even during the inevitable
misfortunes that afflict mortal life.

Jesus said to His followers who were arguing about their
respective greatness: "If any one wants to be first, he must
make himself last of all and servant of all." (Mark 9:35) If we
want to share the good news with those outside our circle, we
must follow the call of the Holy Spirit to communicate
joyously with the wretched of the earth, to bind up the
broken-hearted, to proclaim liberty to the captives, and to
release those in prison, as is said in Isaiah 61:1. The captives
are those who are enslaved to the things of this world and the
opinions of other people; the prison is our own mind, where
we constantly re-live old patterns of thought or rehearse past
scores against those who may have hurt us many years ago.
People who live in a past world of resentment do not realise
that time has gone by and that the years have brought a
degree of maturity to all concerned. In all probability those
against whom they bear a grudge are now as responsible in
their outlook and as tortured in their sensitivity as they are

themselves. Only the greater love of God brought to such warped souls by the presence and actions of those whose lives are devoted to Him can unlock the prison of the unconscious and free the person from the captivity of past memories.

It is customary in the present climate of thought to interpret captivity and imprisonment in political and social terms, but the truly spiritual person knows that all enslavement begins in the person, from whom it proceeds into perverse social and economic action. No wonder Jesus condemned those who cleaned the outside of cup and dish while the inside was left full of robbery and self-indulgence. (Matthew 23:25) Those who attempt with arrogant self-assertiveness to put the world aright should look at themselves first. "Why do you look at the speck of sawdust in your brother's eye, with never a thought for the great plank in your own? Or how can you say to your brother, 'Let me take the speck out of your eye', when all the time there is a plank in your own? You hypocrite! First take the plank out of your own eye, and then you will see clearly to take the speck out of your brother's." (Matthew 7: 3-5) If only the political idealists and dogmatic religionists would heed Jesus' words, we might begin to see heaven created on our solid earth!

These are some of the ways in which the gospel is proclaimed and the reality of Christ brought into the lives of men, even if they refuse to acknowledge His name directly.

In Carl Jung's autobiography, *Memories, Dreams, Reflections*, his therapeutic ethos is stated as follows:– "I never try to convert a patient to anything, and never exercise a compulsion. What matters most to me is that the patient should reach his own view of things. Under my treatment a pagan becomes a pagan, and a Christian a Christian, a Jew a Jew, according to what his destiny prescribed for him." This dispassionate view of the relativity of belief cannot be expected to please a dogmatic follower of a particular religion who has no doubt that his scheme of salvation is the only right one. But Jung is nearer the truth than such a person, and he has in practice been a finer agent of healing than the great majority of protagonists of religion of whom I am aware. We must eschew the ego-inflating temptation of trying to convert a person to our beliefs; we must do all in our power to help him become an authentic human being. This is a hard saying for those whose religion is imbued with a strong missionary commitment. In fact, this point of view does not diminish our duty to mission; on the contrary, it sharpens it and makes it a spiritual task with a healing basis. But the mission is to heal a broken world and revive a flagging people, not to enrol large numbers of people into a particular religious denomination.

What I am saying is this: the word *salvation* should be interpreted in terms of bringing the soul — and indeed the whole person — to a state of health, or wholeness. The concepts of salvation as the deliverance of the person from sin and its consequences so that he can be saved from the torments of hell and gain admission to heaven, is a negative approach to the healing process and gives priority to the fear of God's wrath rather than the wonder of His unremitting love. Those who can lead a person to greater health are those who will spread their gospel most convincingly. They will have no need of coercion to bring others to a spiritual understanding. On the other hand, those who have been brought to healing by them will demand to know their secret. This is how humility works to the glory of God, while arrogant claims merely estrange the sensitive and the intelligent from contact with spiritual things.

All of us who are aware of spiritual reality desire above all else to bring our brothers to the light. But we must beware lest our zeal excludes the Holy Spirit, Who alone can effect the sudden change in consciousness that is the basis of a real conversion, or turning to the light. Revivalistic techniques work on the emotions of psychologically unbalanced people, and can certainly effect mass conversions to a sectarian view of God, but this harvest of converts should not blind us to the inadequacy of the spiritual outlook evoked in those who declare themselves for God. Those people are sick in spirit. While there is none among us who could claim a perfect bill of spiritual health — for each of us has his own deficiency which prevents him being a whole person — there is at least a tendency amongst those guided by the Holy Spirit to grow into the light of God's love. Those people who are converted to a faith by the experience of being delivered from the wrath to come by personal commitment to a God whose chief attribute is power, tend to remain spiritually sick. Their inner balance depends on a particular doctrinal formulation that does not change in emphasis, and they remain arrogant, intolerant protagonists of a faith that does not grow. They cannot bear the searing fire of the Holy Spirit Who enters the depths of our being and opens up the dark places of the unconscious. Fortunately the Holy Spirit does often make His presence felt in such people, when circumstances in their lives effect a subtle change in their consciousness. Some may have to experience a complete loss of "faith" before they can come to God in love and peace. Others who are more fortunate gradually leave behind the imprisoning doors of compulsive (and compulsory) belief in a particular doctrinal position, and grow progressively into that inner freedom which is the criterion of true spirituality, for "where the Spirit of the Lord is, there is liberty." (2 Corinthians 3:17)

Can an acknowledgement of the sanctity of the human will and conscience be reconciled with a commitment to bring people to Christ? I believe this is the only full commitment, but Christ is larger than the mind of man. Indeed, we all have to enter the mind of Christ through grace effected by the inspiration of the Holy Spirit. If, to return to Jung's therapeutic ethos, a pagan were to become an authentic pagan he would at least bear witness to the four cardinal virtues — fortitude, justice, prudence and temperance. As he progressed in his own life, so the three evangelical virtues — faith, hope and love — would become more urgent, and finally he would know the authentic Christ within himself. The same argument would hold for those who are committed to a higher religion, for as they became more complete people, so they would know the supremacy of the Christ within Who was revealed outwardly in the form of the man called Jesus. And those who proudly call themselves Christians would need to undergo exactly the same transformation, for not everyone who calls Jesus "Lord" will enter the kingdom of Heaven, but only those who do the will of God.

The terrible history of Christian persecution and fratricidal strife emphasises this truth far too eloquently for any complacency on the part of those who minister through Christ to the world. The world does not yet know Christ, although isolated saints of all the great religious traditions have had communion with Him. St John says in his first letter (3:2), "Here and now, dear friends, we are God's children; what we shall be has not yet been disclosed, but we know that when it is disclosed we shall be like Him, because we shall see Him as He is." He goes on to say, "Everyone who has this hope before him purifies himself, as Christ is pure." The way of purification is ceaseless prayer, for the agent of purity is the Holy Spirit and not our own selfish wills trying to make ourselves outwardly presentable to God, while within we contain a cesspit of evil desires and selfish motives.

The true Christ who shows us the way to the Father is one Who gives up His life for the world, Who humbles himself to take on the ignominy of the meanest criminal, Who experiences the tortures of the damned. He is the Spirit of humility. No one comes to God except by the way that He revealed when He was with us in the flesh.

The call is always the same. It is "Follow me".

13

The Fulfilling Spirit

Then a shoot shall grow from the stock of Jesse, and a branch shall spring from his roots. The spirit of the Lord shall rest upon him, a spirit of wisdom and understanding, a spirit of counsel and power, a spirit of knowledge and the fear of the Lord. (Isaiah 11: 1-2)

THE HUMAN BEING functions on three levels: the physical, the psychical, and the spiritual. None is more important than the other, since each is a composite part of the whole, which is the full person. Spirituality is concerned with the bodily organism, which is the temple of the Holy Spirit and a thing of great intrinsic sanctity. It is also concerned with the psychic connexion that unites the parts of a body into a person, the person into a community, and the community into the full body of Christ that is seen completed in the Communion of Saints. But the apogee of spirituality is communion with God. From this emanates the energising power that sanctifies the psychic realm and the physical world. The Word made Flesh demonstrates this three-fold holiness. The spiritual aspect of man must therefore be granted priority but not greater regard than the other parts of his personality.

The full manifestation of the Spirit in man must infuse every cell of his body — indeed every atom — with a heightened vitality, every thought with illuminated understanding, and every emotional response with the deepest caring for others. A new creation can alone contain the full downpouring of the Spirit of God. This Spirit heralds and proclaims a physical transfiguration of the body. The mental inspiration of the Spirit endows the psyche with vast intuitive glimpses of a reality of a very different order from the wildest speculations of the human mind. Its emotional cleansing effect leads to a birth of true spiritual awareness of which the gifts of the Spirit mentioned in 1 Corinthians 12 are a part, albeit only a presage of the glory to be revealed in man.

It cannot be repeated too often that the Holy Spirit effects a renewal of the whole person. The charismatic function mentioned above is only one feature of a much greater inner transformation; it leads to increased psychic sensitivity and power. Those who are ignorant of psychic matters avoid the use of that word, which they erroneously equate with evil, demonic influences. However, an awakening of the psychic senses without a corresponding heightening of the intellectual faculty and a deepening of the awareness of God can easily become demonic inasmuch as the psychic powers are concentrated on the person possessing them rather than bequeathed to God's service in love for one's fellow creatures. This is a hazard of confronting those enthusiasts who equate charismatic gifts with the full working of the Holy Spirit instead of putting these gifts in perspective as one particular grace from God for those who are dedicated in their service to Him.

If the Spirit is working fully, there is an intellectual enlightenment which shows itself in an ability to explore new avenues of thought. Furthermore, the natural state of isolation is relieved and the enclosure of limited self-awareness opened by the inflow of love that comes from God, for "we love because He loved us first". This love casts out fear. Whoever claims the inspiration of the Holy Spirit should have passed beyond the slavery of fear of any principality or power, either temporal or psychic. In the life of the Spirit there is eternal truth, which cannot be dulled by any power, whether physical, intellectual, or even demonic.

There are some religious groups who wage a constant war on what they regard as the demonic powers that influence the world. These people are usually unaware that most of the demonic forces originate from within themselves and are then projected on to any person or group to whom they feel antagonistic. In the end all those who disagree with them are identified with the devil and his works. Many such deluded people are in fact abnormally sensitive psychically, but have not come to terms with their own condition or analysed their impressions dispassionately. If they had the courage and the intelligence to do this, they would realise that most of the demonic forces they encountered were part of the spirit of fear and ignorance that pervades the world and is dominating their own consciousness.

By contrast, the person genuinely inspired by the Holy Spirit, while never oblivious of the demonic dimension of reality, is not overwhelmed by it. He knows how to deal with the dark forces in the world and in himself, quietly, unemotionally, and effectively. Indeed, in collaboration with this work of the Holy Spirit man attains the peak of his nobility. We must strive not merely to check and neutralise the dark forces but to use their impetus for good. This is why a Spirit-filled person's level of awareness is raised far above the lower reaches of the unconscious, where the demonic elements are to be encountered, to the higher planes where he is in full relationship with his fellow men and also with the Communion of Saints. In other words, the Spirit effects a progressive raising of the consciousness of the person whom He infuses. It is centred no longer on the personal self or the impulses serving the self, but is concentrated on God and the service due to Him. It must be noted, however, that in the new awareness of reality, neither the personal self nor its "lower" impulses of preservation, procreation, and assertion are ignored or dismissed. On the contrary, they are acknowledged with thanksgiving, but they cease to be the centre of influence of the person. Instead they are preserved under the guardianship of a newly-raised self that is closer to God.

The self is, as I have already indicated, the focus of personal consciousness. It has to die daily in order to be renewed and raised from the death of selfishness to the life of God. The self is not annihilated in the spiritual life; it is so transformed that the final product can hardly be related to the primitive source of its origin. The end of this is St Paul's exultant cry: "The life I now live is not my life, but the life which Christ lives in me." (Galatians 2:20) The Spirit has done His work when the seed of God, the Word deeply placed in the soul of man, germinates and grows to become the tree of life, which is the true vine described in the fifteenth chapter of St John's Gospel. Then Christ is shown to be all because He is assuredly in all.

The raising of consciousness is a theme widely current in contemporary thought. There are many techniques of meditation canvassed by enthusiasts that aim at achieving a raised consciousness, and it is possible that some even succeed for a time. But the meditator soon lapses into the old way of semi-awareness, because his personality has not been made holy. It remains unredeemed, although in some instances the psychic faculty is released and the meditator may become aware of principalities hidden from other people. But this in itself is as likely to be deleterious as beneficial to his spiritual development. Psychic irruptions into full consciousness are seldom beneficial until such time as the point of full consciousness has become centred on a greater reality than the unredeemed personal self. When one's life is centred on the theme of service and the Person of the Incarnate Lord, then psychic revelations can be properly assimilated and their import used constructively in the life of the person. This point applies equally to the gifts of Spirit — they cease to be "natural" and become truly charismatic only when the person lives the "risen life" of aspiration in Christ. And this, as I have already stated, demands intellectual and spiritual renewal as well as psychic release.

The raising of consciousness is effected in slow degrees by the Spirit, but sometimes there is a much greater, dramatically sudden opening of awareness so that the totality of existence may be momentarily revealed. This is the basis of mystical experience, in which God is known directly. The knowledge of God is not by intellectual understanding but by direct union with Him. It is not dissimilar to the true knowledge we may gain of someone close to us in a relationship. At first we see him from afar in terms of his outer appearance and his work in the world. We may admire his character and extol his excellent attributes. But when we come closer to him all these facets fall away, and the person becomes more naked to our inner scrutiny. We cease to regard him as a particular individual with gifts, powers, and attributes, but instead begin to feel him as a person. His stature in the world's eyes, or even in our own rational appraisal, becomes increasingly irrelevant. It is what he is as a representative of God's creation in the form of a person that matters. Steadily we come to know his coming and his going, his response and his withdrawal, his affection and his aversion, until we are able to respond intuitively to his presence. When there is complete union of regard — and how beautiful is the archaic way of expressing perfect sexual union as one person's knowledge of another — each loses the self in the other. Arising like a phoenix from this sacrifice, a new creation emerges, a creation that owes its conception to the birth of the Seed Who is Christ in the soul of each lover. The form that this creation assumes may be a human personality conceived by the power of the Holy Spirit or it may be an intuitive glimpse into the full reality of life, which is made real by a renewed dedication and a heightened sense of endeavour.

If this manifestation of the divinity that lies hidden in the soul of each one of us can follow perfect union of one person with another, how much more wonderful is the knowledge that God vouchsafes us when we are sufficiently lifted in awareness to be with Him in the fellowship of unitive love. He lifts the veil that the world of multiplicity has knit around us, preventing us seeing the full reality for the complexity of its parts. Beyond that cloud of confusion there shines the light of eternal order; on the far side of the cloud of unknowing there awaits a vision of beatific reality; transcending the multitude of forms and aspects there is a unity of regard that binds together all pieces, all individuals, all contradictions into a coherent whole, the cementing power of which is love. In the awakened state of consciousness the Spirit is no longer apart from us and only distantly available; He is known to be the atmosphere around us at this very moment and beyond all time. In truth it is "in Him that we live and move, in Him we exist". Then at last do we know with irrefutable certainty God's will for us. It is that we should be like Him, and to this end He has given us the love that creates and sustains the universe. This love, whose range is beyond understanding, is made available in its totality for each individual creature, so that every one may be raised from glory to glory to attain the pre-ordained, final state of a realised son of God.

It is when we know God in unitive regard that we understand, not only with the reason but with the heart, that love is the supreme property of life, and that its end is man's growth into the corporate unity of God. And yet this growth, though the very purpose of life, requires man's full assent. It is not an automatic process in which the creature is carried along passively. For the creaturely assent there must first be a renewed, redeemed will, a will freed from the slavery of lower personal desires and now set on nothing less than bringing the kingdom of God, which is love, down to the earth. The redemption of the personal will, which is in effect the preliminary work that the Holy Spirit performs in preparation for the divine encounter in man, follows, as we have seen, great personal suffering and the abasement of personal pride in the refining fire of humiliation. Only then can the Word, deeply set in the soul as the Seed of Christ, teach the will discipline as It teaches the personality the meaning of unreserved love. A redeemed will is a glorious testimony to the divine creation. It is free in intent, vibrant in energy, and warm in affection. It is now able to work in harmony with the sanctifying Spirit of God — and as it co-operates with the Spirit and dedicates itself to the world's service, so it attains greater sanctification and glimpses that perfection to which Christ points the way in His command and, above all, in His ministry.

The full impact of the Holy Spirit is known only in direct mystical illumination. Everything that preceded the event of illumination is a preparation for the unitive encounter. Assuredly the Spirit was active in the life of the disciple long before the peak of recognition, but He was effecting preliminary work on the personality. This is where the early stages of exploration into the darkness of the unconscious were of vital importance, so that the cleansing and redemption of all that was awry could be achieved by the forgiving love of God. Likewise the will had to be gradually weaned from the dominance of the self to the dedication of the self to God — seen above all in service to one's fellows. And the psychic faculty needed to be cleared of personal illusion, so that it could become a transparent, pellucid medium of communication between the Holy Spirit and the person, embracing the full Communion of Saints in its extent.

When "this thing of darkness I acknowledge mine" — and acknowledging it I love it — when it is "thy will not mine be done", when the media of psychical communication are cleared of all interference and illusion, only then can the soul accommodate, indeed tolerate, the full effulgence of the Holy Spirit. This is the reason why self-transcending experience can never be cultivated. To be sure, it is possible to force the portals of a realm of transcendent knowledge by selfish means, notably drugs and meditation techniques, but the inflow of psychic energy into the exposed personality is so great that the person cannot cope with it. He is dislodged from his present point of worldly identity before he has attained a spiritually based knowledge of eternal values. He is afforded a glimpse of the greater vision of mystical union without being shown how to attain it, and at the same time the solid foundations of his present situation are dangerously undermined. He lives in a shadow-world in which fleeting appearances are confused with ultimate reality, and his sense of inner authenticity is disrupted without any more durable focus of reality being available to replace it.

In other words, those who gain illicit entrance to the transcendent mode of being, do so at the cost of their firm base in the temporal mode. They flounder perilously in a fathomless ocean of desolation from which they can occasionally glimpse a greater reality but are powerless to attain it. There is a vast gulf separating the self-transcendent mode, that is eternal life, from the earth-bound dimension of personal identity. One alone unites them, being at once bridge, ferry-man, and guide — the Holy Spirit. He alone, as the guide to the Word within, can bring the soul to a full knowledge of the new way. Those who attempt the lonely journey to spiritual awareness without the motivation of love and service but intent only on their own development, will never reach the promised land until they have come to a knowledge of their own darkness and impotence and are able to call on the name of God in the deepest prayer. Before this can be achieved, they may well have had to experience complete dereliction.

Here indeed is a modern version of the Parable of the Prodigal Son in which the youth attempts the perilous journey to ultimate knowledge without first dedicating himself to God, Who is known to the aspiring mind as a trinity of love, truth, and beauty. Such a person has shown commendable enterprise and exemplary courage, but has unfortunately lacked humility. This comes with the dereliction; only then can the Prodigal Son return to God and learn the true way to self-transcendence, which is service to others, love of all creatures, and an unflinching self-knowledge in which, as I have already mentioned, the dark unconscious, the will, and the psychic faculty are cleansed, renewed, and sanctified by the Holy Spirit. One can only comment with wry humour that the various schools of occult spiritual development that are so popular nowadays have the ultimate effect of bringing the aspirant to the original point of his departure, albeit an older, wiser person. Therefore even in this there is the finger of God's providence.

In contrast with the ill-advised occultist who has forced an entry to the world of spiritual reality and has sustained psychological imbalance and psychic invasion as a result of his impropriety, the true mystic moves to an ever-increasing personal integration as the result of the healing influence of the Holy Spirit. The validity of a self-transcending experience is the extent to which it leads the subject beyond self-concern to self-dedication and eventually self-sacrifice in an act of love for the brethren. The more full one is of the power of the Holy Spirit, the emptier is one of self-regard. The reason for this is not that the self is banished and destroyed, but that it is fulfilled and spiritualised. The true self, which is the heart of a person and identified most nearly as the soul, has at last appeared in full consciousness, no longer concealed beneath the clouds of unresolved conflicts that normally darken the unconscious. At last the personal self of everyday life is at one with the true being of the person, and his point of awareness has been raised from his own sensations, which fluctuate minute by minute, to an identification with the whole world of which he is now in truth an integral, coherent part.

The fruit of spiritual identity is joy; it is the expression of the Spirit deeply placed in the soul, which in the natural state of consciousness is unfortunately hidden by the outer cares of the person. When the identity of the self has been raised to the spiritual dimension, joy radiates from the person like the sun's rays suddenly shining through a clear chink of sky between dissipating clouds. This joy is the product of the confirmation not only of the soul's unique identity, but of its eternity — that it can never be destroyed even if the world around it is falling into chaos. The effect this realisation has on one's relationships with others is revolutionary. One depends no more on the support of any person, because one knows that the support which sustains the centre of one's life comes from the Holy Spirit. He fills the soul with life eternal and illuminates it with light that has no secondary source, but is the uncreated, primal, outflowing energy of God. Depending on no one and being immutably fixed in the centre where the will of God directs one about one's work, one is in creative relationship with everyone. Some respond harmoniously and are well disposed; others cannot comprehend the light and power that proceed from the spiritually integrated person and seek to thwart his works and finally to destroy him. But above and beyond this vortex of conflicting human emotions, unformed and inchoate, the soul of the illuminated one is in communion with God and the company of Saints in the life eternal; and it is His privilege to further the kingdom of God in the intermediate psychic realms and the material earthly ones. This is the consciousness of the Transfigured Christ, at one with the source of law and prophecy, and yet at the same time in the world surrounded by devoted, yet ignorant disciples and the dark powers of negation intent on destroying Him. Beyond time and in time simultaneously, He redeems time in eternity by His living sacrifice to the world of time. In the Transfiguration the point of time and space which is marked by a living body is raised to its origin in the world of eternal values. The Spirit has commenced His great work of raising corruptible matter, subject to all the changes of each moment in space, to incorruptible spirit where it is fit to partake fully of the divine nature to which it is heir.

This is true communion, to be in fellowship with all men — and indeed the whole creation — in the conscious presence of God. This is the full meaning of heaven. One is present everywhere at the same time so that even when one is absent in the body, one is available in the spirit. There are no demands and no expectations set on anyone in the divine community, because there is that total trust which accompanies complete openness. Thus it was in Eden before the insolence of natural human awareness had set itself apart from the totality of creation to acquire knowledge for its own advantage. At that fateful moment of isolated self-recognition, humanity realised its own nakedness, and in the fear that accompanies pride hid from the one Source Who could have clothed the flesh in transfiguring radiance. What we call the Fall was the beginning of man's journey to self-awareness, but the suffering he has inflicted on the world in the process of his self-realisation is beyond measure. Only the Incarnation could reconcile man once more with the Source of his being, and demonstrate how self-mastery is achieved only in communion with God. In this revelation a new heaven was opened to mankind, and indeed it was the abode of the earliest Christian disciples despite the severe persecution levelled against them by the secular arm.

It was the tragedy of Ananias and Sapphira that they preferred limited possession of half-bequeathed money to the open sharing of a heavenly community. When one enters a new way of life, one cannot obstruct the flow of the Holy Spirit with impunity. (Acts 5: 1-10)

The fire of the Spirit in the heavenly realm, whether in a divinely appointed community on earth or in the life beyond death, is so fierce and consuming of all dross that only the transfigured ones can hope to survive in it. It is on this account that those who are rich in their own conceit cannot enter the kingdom of heaven. I cannot personally believe that Ananias and Sapphira were permanently lost — any more than I can bear the thought that any of God's creatures could be totally annihilated — but it is evident that they forfeited their places in that divine community by their inability to give of themselves fully. Thus many are called, but few chosen in any generation.

These teachings about the divine community are brought out in Jesus' ministry. Early on, it is recorded that His family set out to take charge of Him because people were saying that He was out of His mind. (Mark 3:21) When He was told that His mother and brothers had arrived and wanted Him to come out to them, He asked "Who is my mother? Who are my brothers?" He went on to say that whoever did the will of God was His brother, sister, or mother. (Mark 3: 31-35) This approach to personal relationships is re-echoed in His teaching about the resurrection of the dead. "When they rise from the dead, men and women do not marry; they are like angels in heaven." (Mark 12:25) None of this is meant as a denigration of personal relationships. The discipline of a loving marriage is a crucial way of spiritual development for the great majority of people. In such a relationship one's own shortcomings are pitilessly laid bare, while at the same time one gradually learns the lessons of patience and forbearance in respect of the other person. But in only a few such marriages is there that degree of trust and mutual self-giving that allows each to grow fully into a person and give of himself or herself unreservedly to the greater world also in loving service. That is why at a certain stage there must be a severance of the physical relationship no matter how rewarding it may have been, so that each can grow even more fully into personal identity in the silence of bereavement. The end of this is the establishment of a new intensity of relationship with the greater body of one's fellows, while at the same time being in a closer, non-sensual communion with the loved one beyond death.

In the spiritual life there is a fellowship that transcends merely personal needs and embraces the whole world in its caring. This is how chastity should be understood. Far from being an escape from self-commitment in personal relationships, it is the way of total self-giving in all relationships, so that no one person is elevated above the other in the esteem of the one who ministers to them all. Chastity sanctifies every personal relationship and blesses it so that it ceases to be a merely temporary event but assumes the quality of eternity. Chastity exalts the person in the glory of his uniqueness, whereas promiscuity degrades the person by levelling him to his place as one of an infinite series of objects to be used for selfish motives.

The risen life of the Spirit exalts each individual to his fully unique stature, and it is consummated in a union of the one with the many in which each attains and proclaims the integrity of a proper person by shedding his isolation in the fellowship of the whole. In this fellowship death is seen to be an insubstantial shadow, eternally traversed by the shafts of loving light that proceed from one person to another. As the angelic hosts move about their appointed work in effortless precision, so do those who live in heaven relate to each other as they go about God's business of raising the spiritually dead to a new vision of transfigured glory.

14

Transfiguration

Six days later Jesus took Peter, James, and John with him and led them up a high mountain where they were alone; and in their presence he was transfigured; his clothes became dazzling white, with a whiteness no bleacher on earth could equal. (Mark 9: 2-3)

THE TRANSFIGURATION OF the body is the consummation of the action of the Holy Spirit in the world. That corruptible matter, by its very nature evanescent and perishable, may finally assume the quality of eternal spirit is the meaning of life, the end to which growth proceeds, and the goal of all separative existence through the miasma of suffering and illusion. It is the destiny of the physical body to become the living temple, not made by hands or even the atoms of material substance, of the Holy Spirit. Such a transformed body ceases to be imprisoned in a world governed by the forces that lead to death and corruption; it is no longer merely an edifice of flesh and bone, but becomes shot through with a vibrancy of life that is generated from a spring deep within it that is also one with the eternal life that proceeds from the reality of God. And so the physical body itself is no longer limited in extent by the external dimensions it presents to the world. When it is transfigured, the sanctifying power of the Holy Spirit extends its nature to participate in the fullness of the whole created universe. It is included in the greater communion of the cosmos by the life it shares in common, a life no longer separate and apparently isolated from the whole, but instead fully awakened, responsive and loving. Thus it comes about that the flesh which once reacted passively to the life that flowed through it, and was dense, opaque and uncomprehending, is now active with renewed life, vibrant in joyful self-affirmation, and outflowing in vigour to the world around it. Its constituent cells, indeed the very atoms that compose them, send forth a radiance that proclaims their own intrinsic transformation, and also prefigures the integrating influence the transfigured body will exert on the awakening world around it. For indeed, the outer world is transfigured by the Holy Spirit that proceeds from the glorified body of an illuminated person. This transfigured body is at once in communion with the psychic stratum of the universe and is also the means of liberation of the psychic world from the misty half-lights of illusion to the radiant clarity of the uncreated light of God. For God is light, and in Him there is no darkness at all. (1 John 1:5)

The transfigured Christ is in visible fellowship with the psychic dimension of reality, and indeed raises it from multiplicity to the unity of spiritual encounter. He is in manifest union with the risen Moses and Elijah, who symbolise respectively the eternal law that governs the cosmos and the outflowing prophetic function that leads the cosmos in the way of its own sanctification by the power of the Holy Spirit. This Spirit is eternally making all things new, as He brings the world ever closer to the truth, a truth which the unsanctified world cannot bear to learn. Christ both completes and fulfils the law and leads prophecy to its own end in the perfection of the world and the divinisation of the material universe. And yet Christ remains in fellowship with His three disciples, who for a brief period are raised beyond the horizon of earthly sight so that they can see heavenly things. Frail as they are, and soon to desert their Master when He needs their support most urgently, they too are enveloped in the light of God, and experience a transformation of awareness and possibly even of bodily function. In being released from the bondage of material illusion, they enter into a direct knowledge of the world of eternal values that is the reality underlying all created things. Prophecy and law are fulfilled in the Word of God Who also fulfils the calling of humanity, so that all are united in one light, and those who come after Him can partake of that light and glimpse their way to full union with God.

When the Master and His three disciples descend from the mountain and enter the domain of earthly consciousness, which is under the dominion of the dark forces of selfishness and negation, He warns them to tell no one of what they have witnessed until the Son of Man has risen from the dead. After transfiguration comes the greatest, indeed the final challenge; to bring the transfiguring light down to earth so that it also may be changed. And we know that the darkness of material inertia cannot understand the light that transfigures. Indeed, it is in perpetual conflict with it until it is changed by a power that acts in weakness. The light can never finally be overcome, although for a brief period it does appear to have waned almost to the point of extinction.

When Moses received the Law from God on Mount Sinai, as he was returning to his compatriots below, he was told to make the pieces of the temple according to the design he was shown on the mountain. (Exodus 25:40) This is the acid test of a true mystical experience, one in which the Spirit of God infuses the very marrow of the person, so that the power of God not only transforms his body and mind but renews his will and re-dedicates his soul. Nothing less than the re-creation of the world in the divine image will satisfy him. And yet he knows of how little account he is personally except as an instrument of the grace that proceeds from God. As the personal self is subjugated in God's service, so it is experiencing rebirth. As it dies joyfully to itself, so it is transfigured to an exquisite beauty beyond mortal knowing, and finds its identity in the living fellowship of all creatures to whom it dedicates itself in self-giving love. It dies to the world of selfish concern and justification based on works, and enters a new world of living relationship with God. Indeed, the whole personality is transfigured until it becomes a witness to the indwelling presence of God. As the personal self dies, so the true, spiritual self is able to irrupt through the outer shell of the personality and transform the whole person. The moment of birth of a full person is the point of transfiguration of the personal self so that in ceasing to be limited to the individual, it becomes a focus of radiant illumination for the whole world. It is now that the individual graduates to the full status of a person, at one even with the Persons of the Holy Trinity.

The full effect of transfiguration becomes, of course, only gradually apparent in the outer life of the person. The climactic events in the life of Christ represent an urgent acceleration of spiritual activity occurring within the framework of a unique man within a few years. In the more usual sequence of spiritual ascent, the adaptation of the psychophysical organism to the intensity of penetration of the energies of the Holy Spirit is gradual but progressive. There is first of all a physical change apparent to those endowed with the gifts of spiritual discernment. This in fact amounts to the ability to see clearly (which is what clairvoyance means) by resting the attention in one-pointed dedication on the matter in hand. If indeed we could only learn to use our five physical senses in serenity and without distraction, these same senses would soon be endowed with a psychic extension that could lead us into a heightened relationship with our own departed and with the world around us. Yet paradoxically this heightened awareness of the senses attains full authority only after the person has been transfigured; only then do the senses attain that degree of illumination by which they can interpret material phenomena in a psychical context, and at the same time raise the phychical element to spiritual completion.

We must remember that the spiritual dimension is the only fully real one inasmuch as it transcends space and time in eternal union with God. The psychical dimension is subject to the influence of the emotion and will of all sentient creatures (including the intermediate angelic hierarchy) and is therefore subject to change and obfuscation, a situation that is inherent in the physical world, which, in our present dispensation, moves inevitably to decay by what physicists would call the law of entropy and by what all creatures know as the law of death. This law is the wages of the sinful, separative existence of the material creation unredeemed by the love that comes only from a knowledge of God.

The physical change apparent in the transfigured person is an increased transparency of the body. Saints have been depicted traditionally as surrounded by an iridescent halo, which is especially apparent around the head. Those who are gifted with clairvoyance describe an 'aura' around the bodies of all people, and they claim to be able to discern not only the physical state of the person by the radiance and colour of the aura, but also the degree of intellectual attainment and the spiritual stature. Of the validity of this gift I have no doubt, and it can be of service to those engaged in counselling and the ministry of healing. But it is essentially a gift of psychic discernment, useful if employed with reverence, but easily becoming a dangerous distraction when invested with personal glamour and sensationalism, as is unfortunately the rule with psychic gifts that are not spiritually grounded.

In any case the transparency of a transfigured person is something apart from the investing auric emanation. It would seem as if the uncreated light, which is the emergent energy of the Godhead, penetrates the physical body, dissipating its opacity and lightening its gravity, so that it assumes a diaphanous consistency. From it there radiates a warmth, which is loving kindness, and a light, which is faithful assurance, that penetrate the hard core of the outside world and re-animate the dull, uncomprehending people in the vicinity. The transparency testifies to the person's sanctity. It has the effect of laying him open to the deepest scrutiny of other people, and the sensitivity that is thereby engendered brings with it a searing vulnerability. The transfigured person is as naked to the vision of man as were his primal ancestors, Adam and Eve, before they chose the divergent path of selfish attainment and separative knowledge that excluded them from the unitive knowledge of God. In their new relationship with the world, they had chosen independence and selfish knowledge, and at once they became aware of their own incompleteness. The body returns anew to the perfection of its primal, naked innocence when it is clothed in the light that comes from the Holy Spirit. But the way of return is strait and narrow; it is the way of purgation through travail and suffering.

The spiritual light is of a different order from the glitter that sometimes radiates from the surface of people who have a strongly developed, self-centred, psychic presence. Charm exudes from this type of person to the extent of deceiving the people around him. I believe that the light of the evil one, who is called Lucifer, is of this type. It was not always so, for ultimately the uncreated light of God is the source of all radiance. When God said "Let there be light", and there was light, as recounted in the Creation story of Genesis 1:3, His light was then transformed into created light that assumes a psychical and then a physical potency. This created light is under the domination of the creatures of the universe, angelic and demonic (a demon is an angelic presence who has perverted the light of God by serving selfish ends) as well as human.

In itself this light is not merely beneficial but indeed life-giving, but it can be misused for personal power. And then it becomes a force of psychic evil. The evil that proceeds from the demonically possessed person perverts spiritual things; it corrupts noble aspiration by cynicism and despair, and misuses spiritual gifts for personal ends. St Paul says: "For our fight is not against human foes, but against cosmic powers, against the authorities and potentates of this dark world, against the superhuman forces of evil in the heavens." (Ephesians 6:12)

Misused psychic light emanates from evil sources, whether human or demonic. This light, unlike the spiritual light that pervades the body of a saint, tends to separate the individual, defining his distance from those around him, and investing him with a power over others. Far from rendering the individual transparent in simplicity and goodness, it surrounds him with a barely penetrable sheen that occludes the scrutiny of the world, and prevents its gaze penetrating the inner depths of his personality. He becomes invulnerable to criticism levelled against himself, and lacks compassion for his fellows: real vulnerability and compassion are the result of a life spent in communion with one's brethren, especially during the long years of suffering. The false light prevents that person participating fully in the lives of others; it is a measure of his separation from them so that he can use them for his own selfish ends but can never give himself in friendship to them. The perverted psychic light symbolises his isolation; it is also the way that he isolates himself. His stark, selfish power is the means of his downfall. Only when the psychic light is dimmed in personal tragedy, can that same light be changed, by the grace of God, into a transfiguring brightness which redeems and sanctifies his broken body.

The essential quality of transfiguration is openness. This openness is primarily one of receptivity to the Holy Spirit. On the lower level of awareness it includes openness to one's fellows (and their hostile attitudes) and also an openness to the vast potentiality of the cosmos with its mosaic pattern of light and darkness. On the higher level of awareness, it brings with it an openness to God, so that there is a conscious interplay between the Holy Spirit and the personality. The result of this open communication on the level of spiritual awareness is the gift of prophecy, the one that St Paul especially commended and exhorted his disciples to attain. (1 Corinthians 14: 1 and 39)

The true prophet is transfigured by the light of God and becomes a cleansed person. His consciousness is raised far above the normal level of selfish vision to the vision of God. Isaiah's call to prophecy is a classical statement of this truth, and deserves to be studied as a whole. (6: 1-9) He describes his vision of God seated on a throne, high and exalted, in the temple, attended by the highest of the angelic hierarchy who nevertheless cannot bear to face Him directly, so that one pair of wings covers their faces and another their feet, while the third is spread out for flight. They glorify God ceaselessly while the threshold shakes to its foundation and the house is filled with smoke, which signifies the cloud by which God showed Himself to the Israelites during their forty years' journey through the desert to the Promised Land. In this vision of the transcendent God, Isaiah can feel only complete separation because of his own sinfulness and that of the people among whom he dwells, a sinfulness typified by unclean thoughts and words. An angel purifies his mouth with a glowing coal from the altar, which symbolises the destroying fire of the uncreated light of God. This act effects Isaiah's transfiguration, and he can then volunteer to be sent for God's service. When Isaiah says: "Here am I; send me", he is at once not only a full person, but also one both with God and the people to whom he is sent as prophet and healer.

The prophet's life has been changed. He has been moved from the small centre of personal life to the larger centre of God's purpose. To be sure, his personal life is not obliterated; on the contrary, it usually proceeds with increasing suffering, as the history of Jeremiah attests, and yet the prophet has passed beyond the thralldom of private attachments to the service of God and his fellow men, whose demands in obedience and dedication are absolute. Once he has consecrated his life to the Most High, he is assured of such an interior purgation that his suffering mounts in intensity until the self, as it is known here on earth, is completely broken. At that juncture, the prophet discovers who he really is — a son of God returning renewed to the image of God in which he was created. This mystery is revealed by the supreme experience of crucifixion.

Since the prophet is transfigured by the Holy Spirit, he alone can speak the direct word of God, for he has known Him in the depth of his soul. In this divine discourse, even the Communion of Saints are excluded from direct participation, but may well play a secondary role in aiding the prophet in his teaching work. They do not transmit the message as in psychic communication, which, as I have already noted, is liable to misinterpretation and interference both by intermediate psychic presences and the unconscious prejudices of the person who receives the message. It follows that real prophecy is a rare spiritual gift, and of a different order from the rather trivial messages that proceed from the lips of the charismatic person, which are clearly of psychic origin. True prophecy is reserved for those who can bear the searing light of God's revealing truth as well as the burning fire of His purifying love. The prophet's transfigured soul and mind proclaim a truth that changes the course of people's lives, and yet he remains humble in himself, intent only on self-effacement. It is this attitude that is of the greatest importance in distinguishing between the true prophet on the one hand and the transmitter of psychic information on the other. If the psychic transmitter could become selfless in holy living, he would be eligible for transfiguration, according to God's will, and would attain a truly prophetic status.

The prophetic function is essentially an aspect of mystical union with God. Superficially this would appear to be a contradiction in terms, since the essence of prophecy is God's transcendent holiness, His absolute otherness from all His creation, whereas mystical illumination effects union between God and the soul of man. However, the mystic understands, as does no other person, how far above understanding God is, and that any knowledge of God is by loving union, when the personality of the mystic is transformed beyond description to a new focus of being, which is at one with all things. And when the ecstasy of union is passed, the mystic has perforce to return to the world of dark separation in order to redeem it by ardent service. In this serving capacity, the mystic is aware of the uncharted distance, in the realm of values, that separates the Deity from the cosmos. "For my thoughts are not your thoughts, and your ways are not my ways. For as the heavens are higher than the earth, so are my ways higher than your ways and my thoughts than your thoughts." (Isaiah 55:8-9).

It is the responsibility of the mystic to bring down to earth what he has been shown on the mountain of transfiguration. The message is seldom one of earthly comfort, since only a radical change of heart, a complete cleansing from sin (which is the attitude that exalts personal privilege over communal

concern) can save the world from the consequences of
separative existence, which are destruction and death. The
true prophet, like God Whose mouth-piece he is, has no
favourites among the nations. The theological and moral
assessments are international in scope, and the predictions are
beyond the limits of personal preference. In Old Testament
prophecy, the children of Israel are chosen not for worldly
power but to be the special servants of God's grace, to herald
His advent among the nations. And that service brings
suffering, not self-aggrandisement. This lesson is as far from
being understood today as it was in the time that Isaiah 53
was written, or when Jesus demonstrated it in His Passion
some five hundred years later.

Thus Jeremiah can proclaim Nebuchadnezzar, who is to be
the destroyer of Jerusalem and the Temple, as "servant of
God" (27:6). Isaiah can foresee a time when Israel shall rank
with Egypt and Assyria, and these three shall be a blessing in
the centre of the world. So the Lord of Hosts will bless them:
"a blessing upon Egypt my people, upon Assyria the work of
my hands, and upon Israel my possession." (19:24-25) In what
is the peak of Old Testament prophecy, Jeremiah proclaims
the new interior covenant that is to be between God and His
people (31: 31-34). God will set His law within them and
write it in their hearts. They will no longer need to teach one
another to know the Lord, because each will know Him in his
own soul. When God is known with this degree of intimacy,
prophecy becomes widespread, and the soul has experienced
transfiguration.

The openness of the body to the transfiguring power of the
Holy Spirit is the zenith of the healing process. If medical
practice acts on the body, and psychotherapy on the intellect
and emotions, and the laying-on of hands and other charismatic forms of healing on the intricate psychic structure that
energises and interpenetrates the human organism, the power
of the Holy Spirit acts directly on the spirit of man and effects
a dramatic, sometimes instantaneous realignment of the
whole personality. In the annals of spiritual healing there are
well-authenticated instances of people who were ill to the

point of death and completely unresponsive to the medical treatment available to them. When all seemed lost and death was patiently awaited, suddenly new life burst in on the sufferer. He was transfigured and a new potency of energy seemed to flow through his dying body. Like the sufferers in the accounts of Jesus' healing ministry, these people quite literally rose from their agony and took up what seemed destined to be their deathbeds and walked away healed. But what marked their healing as of a different order from the spectacular phenomena that are reported from time to time amongst psychic healers was the radical transformation of their whole personality when they were delivered from sickness and death. Their whole perspective had changed, and from that point onwards the Person of the Risen Christ was the centre and end of their life.

I believe this is the real end of healing, a topic that has been considered on more than one occasion in this account of the work of the Holy Spirit in the life of mankind. The other agencies of healing already mentioned are all of irreplaceable value in their own right, and none is to be relegated to an inferior place. But they act in a secondary capacity, since none alone, or even all acting together, can produce the inner transfiguration that the Holy Spirit freely bestows. Such truly mystical healing is a pure grace of God. Some who have experienced it are deeply believing people whose lives are devoted to Christ. Others are fighting agnostics, far from the Kingdom of God as conceived by the conventional, complacent believer. But God knows the potentiality of the individual soul more intimately than does even its closest mortal friend. Indeed, there are many people whose piety actually separates them from an encounter with God; they fondly believe they are serving God when in fact they have merely succeeded in enslaving themselves to a form of ritual which at the most can help to direct the mind and affections Godward. But in itself it rapidly assumes the power of an idol. When such a deluded person does receive a visitation from the Holy Spirit, all his preconceptions are shattered by a mighty wind, and he is rendered naked as he was before he put on the vesture of intellectual conceit and the armour of dogmatic arrogance.

Healing is gradual: the Spirit has first to release pent up tensions in the unconscious mind and restore the will before the person is able to face the world around him with inner strength and balance. This is the first degree of openness. Then he has to face the tentative nature of all articles of faith and even the exploratory path towards a knowledge of God. This is the second degree of openness — an openness to the inroads of uncertainty and frank doubt in the face of conflicting ideologies and new scientific discoveries, to which active participation in everyday life exposes all preformed belief by the penetrating light of intellectual probity. The end of this openness is a loving acceptance of all men as they are, respecting their diversity of belief and learning from them what is essential to one's own growth into a full person. The third degree of openness is towards the psychic emanations of other people, so that one can give freely of oneself, knowing that in the end betrayal awaits one. This way alone brings with it the knowledge of love, and it is consummated on the Cross of human suffering.

While the redeemed person is growing into a full acceptance of the light of God, which is stark, penetrating, and purifying, that light enters the naked soul and starts the process of transfiguration. What appears to be a sudden irruption of spiritual power into the depths of the person's soul, experienced by him as mystical illumination, is much more probably the fruit of a long period spent in internal development through the testing grounds of self-sacrifice, doubt and humiliation. When the disciple has passed beyond such concerns as his own future, and his deserts, privileges and expectations, and comes to know that living the good life in every moment of time is the meaning and reward of that life, the Spirit is indeed upon him. He has now had the authentic vision of eternal life. It is at this stage of illumination that he can begin to grasp the intention behind the healing process, so that he can at last become an agent of God's full healing power.

From this we can understand how long and arduous is the work of healing. It is not to be forced or accelerated by a human, or even an angelic agent. Its source is God alone, and He knows the right time. The main work of the healer is to sustain the sufferer with constant solicitude and prayer so that he may be given the strength to learn the lessons his malady has to teach him. Before he has understood this and gained the ultimate blessing from wrestling with adversity, the victim may grope from one system of metaphysics to another. But in the end he will know God through his own explorations. "You must work out your own salvation in fear and trembling; for it is God who works in you, inspiring both the will and the deed, for his own chosen purpose." (Philippians 2:13)

Saint Augustine confessed ruefully to praying to God to give him chastity but not yet. And yet that prayer had an inner wisdom despite its apparent immaturity. Until the inner constitution of the saint is ready, it is of no avail for him to assume the burden of a physical and emotional discipline too heavy for him to bear. Those who take on themselves the burden of the ascetic life before they are ready for it, will bring on themselves a multitude of psychological ills and psychic obsessions. This is why piety, puritanism, and religiosity are all potentially demonic attitudes. What the devotee has consciously rejected in the name of God comes back to him by way of the unconscious. Unable to accept the threat of its truth in his own life, he promptly projects it on the people in his vicinity, on those who differ from him in religious belief, and especially on the stranger in his midst. No agency in human life bears a greater responsibility for the cruelty of persecution than do the religions of the world; the theistic group bear a special blame because of the narrow, dogmatic approach they so often display to the Ultimate Reality Whom men call God — personal and transpersonal, beyond all knowing and yet close to the child in loving union. On the other hand, when the disciple has learned the lessons that everyday life has to teach him — devotion to the common duties of the passing hour, probity in personal

relationships, patience in the face of provocation, perseverance when every circumstance is adverse and all seems to be
futile, compassion to the uncomprehending and jealous, love
to every living creature — then he will have reached that
inner simplicity which shows itself outwardly in an austere
style of living.

This type of ascetic life is no burden; it is unbounded joy,
for one is no longer attached to the things of this world, but
can see them as a way to eternal union with God. When one
has passed beyond the need for any thing (or person), only
then can one be in perpetual relationship with all things (and
people). This is the life of heaven for which we are preparing
as we move "in fear and trembling" to do God's business,
which is to seek our own salvation and bring salvation to all
creation also, through the power of the Holy Spirit that
proceeds from God's Word deeply placed in the human soul.

15

Confrontation

The hour has come. The Son of Man is betrayed to sinful men. Up, let us go forward! My betrayer is upon us. (Mark 14: 41-42)

THE END OF the spiritual life is failure, not the shoddy success that the world esteems. The final manifestation of the Holy Spirit in the life of man is destruction of all he has held dear and sacrosant, not the preservation of temporal values and pious attitudes. The Spirit, if He is allowed free rein over a man, demands a new creation, not a patching-up and adornment of the present life. Whoever believes that the final good can be equated with heaven on earth, whether on a political, economic, social, or even religious dimension, is not aware of the meaning of the Holy Spirit. Indeed, heaven and earth, as we know them, have to pass away before the Word of God can be finally revealed in the deepest layer of the created universe.

Anyone who looks for comfort and reassurance in worldly things is living in an illusion. The world is in fact tolerable, indeed beautiful, only to him who has overcome that world and can enjoy it with a degree of non-attachment that does not flinch from the possibility of its complete annihilation. Only when one loves a person with that intensity of non-attachment that the prospect of his death becomes a source of comfort and strength, rather than one of intolerable grief, has one come to a knowledge of his eternal value.

All this was hinted at long ago by the Speaker (or Preacher) who summoned forth the inspirational book of Ecclesiastes. To those with a consciousness rooted in earthly things, it is a composition of cynicism, gloom and ultimate resignation to the fact of fate's unpredictability, man's frailty and death's finality. To those with a heavenly awareness, this book is a glimpse of the ultimate release man is to enjoy from the slavery of worldly things, to a realm where neither fate, frailty, nor death has dominion, and where the bliss of eternal communion with all things in a transfigured mode is to be known. Agony is the final result of a life devoted to the accretion of finite things; joy often follows their complete demolition. But the quality that has to be absolutely demolished is the present domination of the self. Its transfiguration is an important stage in that development; its apparent annihilation is the necessary ordeal before it is born anew. It is for this reason that death in all its forms is as essential for the well-being of the soul as is material life.

Death is a stage in the development of a living creature in which it is obliged to renounce its present mode of life and enter an unknown existence, of whose reality the intellect can give little assurance and whose continuity is at best a shadow cast by thoughts in the night. In what we are pleased to call "the lower forms of life", death is seen only at the termination of that life. But man dies day by day if he is living properly. For him death is the continual renunciation of a present way of viewing reality as he grows into a new awareness of his place in the universe. As fresh demands are made and new insights are given, so he dies to the old and is reborn in the new life.

The young child dies to its enclosed parental solicitude when it enters the competitive life of schooling with its peers. And the mother's close attachment dies with it. If this mutual death fails to occur, the child cannot grow into self-giving relationships with other people, and the mother cannot move beyond the imprisoning bonds of a possessive hold on her child. When a young person leaves home and begins to fend for himself, there is another shared death. The child has broken loose from the moorings of a loving family life, to enter the indifferent sea of adult participation, rivalry, and betrayal. And the parents are moving closer towards their own separation from the child. This is their first real presage of the full death they are, in due course, destined to experience. Every disappointment, every disability, every permanent separation of one friend from another, is of the nature of a small death. Some cannot bear the break with a past hope or relationship, and contract out of life. But those who are strong and imbued with faith will go on living. A part of their life has been destroyed, but a new way of living has been opened to them.

The supreme death that confronts us all while we are still alive in the world is the tragedy of bereavement. When a loved one dies, something deep in us also dies, and a void remains. The one on whom we have greatly depended for emotional sustenance has been taken from us, and a chasm of meaninglessness is all that remains. But if this partial breach of the soul can be healed by the influx of new, more widely based relationships in which service and concern for others rather than personal comfort are the dominant factors, we may start to move beyond death to life even in this world. As St John says, "we know that we have crossed over from death to life, because we love our brothers." (1 John 3:14)

This is the secret. Death means the end of a limited view of life, based on the primacy of our own welfare or that of our immediate circle. The sacrifice is inflicted on us by an apparently indifferent fate; all we have to look upon is a dark void. But it is a living void, a vibrant emptiness, into which much can be placed depending primarily on our own inner attitude. In every person there is set an obscure faith which is fed by a hope that dwells in the soul. This faith, however, becomes a real, living quality only when we have given ourselves, empty and battered, to the future life. This is the act of saving faith that allows the Holy Spirit to enter our life and participate in our spiritual development. The result of this participation is the opening up of new ways and the emergence of potentialities and gifts within us, previously unknown and now slowly brought to light. In truth, death to the old way of life has brought with it a resurrection to a new dimension of living and thinking. Those who have the courage to persist, undergo a subtle inner transformation whereby they are separated from the world of material illusion and grow slowly but inexorably into a life of joy, full of the grace of God.

Let it not be imagined moreover, that the forces that encompass these partial deaths during life are pleasant or benign. They are harsh, invariably bitter, and often vicious. Rivalry, disease, mental breakdown, persecution, bereavement, the collapse of one's dearest hopes due to the betrayal of those whom one regarded as friends, are cruel facts of life. They cannot, indeed must not, be diminished, explained away, or dismissed as illusory products of false thinking. To do this would be a betrayal of all that is noble in human nature. It would also be a betrayal of the dark side of life, which too must be given its weight. Those who speak figuratively of giving even the devil his due are nearer the truth than they are probably aware. We cannot escape the dark, demonic influences that overshadow life in the world of becoming, for they too have their part to play, and until they are acknowledged, there can be no end to darkness, no completion of the suffering of mortal creatures, no victory of immortality over transience.

In the spiritual life that directs the activity of the universe and works for its perfection, there are two reciprocal actions: a downpouring of God's Spirit on to the created world, and the manifestation of that same Spirit in the life of every creature. The Spirit that pours down "from heaven" bathes matter in radiance, infuses it with life, and works to release it from the law of death and corruption that governs all mortal things. The Spirit that manifests itself in the creature works for its perfection, modest in forms of life of lower potentiality, but of the stature of Christ in the human dispensation. Thus there are two directions in which man is "divinised" and the world resurrected, from above downwards and from the depth of the human soul upwards. Illuminated saints of all ages, cultures, and religious traditions have shown the light

within, and their witness has never been obliterated because
the light of the Spirit cannot be extinguished. And yet this
light has been dimmed, at times to a point very near total
extinction, by proceeding generations of those who call
themselves believers and try to follow the way. To be sure,
"The light shines on in the dark, and the darkness has never
mastered it." (John 1:5) But neither has that light ever
overcome the darkness of the world, and the two seem to be
locked in a conflict that has no mortal end.

Times of political enlightenment and religious liberalism
tend to bring in their wake a revolt against the mediocrity
such systems unfortunately seem to engender. Man can never
remain content with a static view of life that prevents the full
flow of the Spirit within him. It was necessary for the
Prodigal Son to leave his rich patrimony behind him and
enter into the degradation of hedonistic existence before he
became a real person who could make his own decision, even
in the most abject humiliation. Times of political repression
and religious authoritarianism, which no one with intelligence could possibly applaud, bring in their turn a generation of heroes who are prepared to sacrifice their lives
for the principles of truth and nobility that are the most
enduring heritage of human history, at once bestial and
Christ-like. History redounds to the memory of these heroes
and pioneers, but who follows them? All too often those who
are centred in selfish concern and are unaware of the greater
demands of life or the potentiality lying deep within mankind.

The remarkable intelligence of the human mind has solved
many scientific problems. Perhaps the most striking advance
is the steady progress against disease that modern medical
research has achieved, so that, at the present time, there is an
increasing number of people who are destined to live to an
extreme old age, a burden on society and a misery to
themselves. They have been prevented from dying mercifully
and have never learned to live constructively. It is a matter of
debate whether the scientific revolution of the past few
hundred years has been a blessing or a curse to mankind.

While no one should deny the benefits that scientific knowledge has bestowed on the world, the more far-seeing of us know that these are essentially peripheral to the goal of man, which in the East would be called "liberation" (from the illusion of a self-centred consciousness) and in the West "salvation" (from a life that is centred in selfishness to the exclusion of man and God). Inasmuch as these great objectives are more easily attained in a body that is well cared for, well nourished and healthy than in one that is degraded, starved and diseased, it can be said that the contemporary concern for social and economic justice and scientific research is well based. But this has been achieved at the cost of individual liberty (which in some countries is absolute) and great suffering to animals, who must necessarily bear the brunt of biological experimentation. It is very unlikely that the light of God will finally transfigure a world in which one form of life is gratuitously sacrificed for the selfish ends of another, which is more advanced intellectually but all too often of rudimentary morality and spirituality.

Do not, however, let it be thought that there are easy solutions to these worldly problems. Indeed, there is no intellectual solution to any of them, and realising this fact has a strangely liberating effect. While extremists, as for instance anti-vivisectionists on the one hand and enthusiastic biological research workers on the other, will denounce each others' views uncompromisingly and often with little real understanding of the complexity of the matter, and the more moderate, constrained majority will look for a middle way in which as little damage is done or pain inflicted as is compatible with furthering the cause of what is generally regarded as human progress, the man of spiritual vision knows that these problems are solved from a different point of vantage altogether. In this respect it usually transpires that people who hold extreme views on any basic issue tend to be emotionally unbalanced; hatred for the protagonists of the practice they denounce is more often the motivating factor in their attitude than compassion for those who suffer under it.

It is also generally true that the large, moderate majority is generally concerned more about salving its own conscience in an uneasy situation, or when faced with shadowy injustice, than in penetrating to the roots of the problem and genuinely initiating a change in policy. It therefore comes about that the rational approach to fundamental problems concerning human welfare stumbles awkwardly on the rocks of prejudice, cowardly expediency, and frank self-interest. And by the very nature of things, it cannot do any other, because the rational faculty is under the domination of the unredeemed personal self. Thus the light flickers on in a worldly society, in some places emitting a diffused glow of dim compassion amid the darkness of human indifference, and elsewhere burning brightly in the souls of individual saints who have sacrificed all thoughts of personal gain for the journey to the vision of God.

In the life of the transfigured one, there comes a final ordeal, the confrontation with naked evil. The unprepared soul rightly flinches from this terrible test, but there is no escape for the soul that bears the light of the Holy Spirit. According to the manner in which the test is concluded, depends the future of the world. Well do we pray, as Jesus taught us: "Do not bring us to the test, but save us from the evil one." (Matthew 6:13) We could not face the impact of concentrated evil in our normal, dimly-aware state of consciousness, for we would be overwhelmed by it. We need God's grace to protect us against the psychic darkness that emanates from the cosmic spheres and is projected into the personalities of receptive human beings. Even so, unspeakably evil things have been done to helpless individuals since the birth of human consciousness, and bestial acts have been perpetrated against racial and religious groups that have, in some instances, led to their annihilation. The manifest triumph of evil over good that occurs in the annals of history from time to time is surely the greatest stumbling-block to a belief in God. To the rational mind there is no God or this God is either impotent or as brutal as the creation He has fashioned. There is certainly no intellectual answer to the fact of evil; there is no theodicy that can justify all the facets of evil action in the world. Yet perhaps we may learn that evil too has its place in the scheme of things for setting man free from the comfortable world of mediocrity to enter into a new phase of consciousness where he is unencumbered with mortal concerns.

In the world we inhabit, a world of form that changes, undergoes corruption, death, and renewal, and that moves to its destiny in unceasing hope of total redemption, we see the process of becoming. It is a dynamic universe; it moves perpetually. There are two basic powers that control the universal flow — a power of good that directs the creation, renewed and transfigured, to union and consummation, and a power of negation, which we call evil, that draws the creation back to the primal chaos that existed when the creation had been decreed, directed and initiated by God's Word through the power of His Spirit. The power that denies is an inevitable by-product of the free will God bestowed on His rational creatures, which, in terms of the world we inhabit and therefore know, means man. Legend speaks of a prior, fateful turning away from God by members of the angelic hierarchy who took upon themselves the power of the psychic dimension and misused it. To me this view is full of meaning, and it emphasises the presence of good and evil, light and darkness, in the psychic as well as the material world. In the world of becoming, the world God created at the dawn of time which emerged in timeless eternity, there is a perpetual interplay and conflict between the power that affirms and the power that denies. This is not Manichaean dualism, which tends to see these two forces as the very basis of reality, but a secondary dualism based on the free choice offered by the one Creator to His creation. And both aspects of this dualism, the darkness as well as the light, are under the dominion of God.

"Where can I escape from thy Spirit? Where can I flee from thy presence? If I climb up to heaven, thou are there; if I make my bed in Sheol, again I find thee...If I say, 'Surely darkness will steal over me, night will close around me', darkness is no darkness for thee and night is as luminous as day; to thee both dark and light are one." (Psalm 139: 7-8 and 11-12)

The same truth is expressed in the Book of the Consolation of Israel written by a disciple of the prophet Isaiah: "I am the Lord, there is no other; I make the light, I create darkness, author alike of prosperity and trouble. I, the Lord, do all these things." (Isaiah 45:7) This disciple had the tragedy of the Babylonian exile with the destruction of Jerusalem on which to meditate. Had it not been for this tragedy, which cost countless lives, a renewed, purified Judaism could not have arisen which not only had its own glory to give the world, but was also to be the author of Christianity and Islam. To Dame Julian of Norwich it was revealed: "It behoved that there should be sin, but all shall be well, and all shall be well, and all manner of thing shall be well." (*Revelations of Divine Love*, Chapter 27). So sin is necessary, and what we call evil plays its part. It cannot be eradicated; it has to be brought into the greater light of reality. The Buddha expressed this in his own way: "Hatred does not cease by hatred; hatred ceases only by love. This is the eternal law." (*Dhammapada* 1:5) It is interesting that the next verse states a truth that at first consideration seems quite remote from its immediate predecessor, but in fact is extremely relevant: "Many do not realise that all must one day die. In those who know this fact, all strife is stilled." In learning how we are to die we come to a knowledge of the ultimate reconciliation of good and evil.

Let us remember finally that Satan plays an important, and by no means isolated, part in the Biblical narrative. It is he who slays Job's past life of reliance on earthly and even religious things so that he can either die or else move to a new understanding of God. It is Satan who acts as adversary to accuse the high priest Joshua before the heavenly tribunal. He is the malevolent angel, who is man's enemy, but he acts in concert with the heavenly host. (Zechariah 3:1-2) The wise, humble man learns more from his enemies than from his friends, because enmity evokes qualities previously latent in the person, whereas friendship, except of the deepest intimacy, tends to stifle weaknesses of character with a veneer of kind words that do not deal with the source of the trouble.

When the Holy Spirit descends on Jesus after His baptism, that same Spirit leads Him into the wilderness to be tempted by the devil. Once again there is a close relationship between God and the devil, a relationship that reaches full tension at the time of the Crucifixion. We would do well to penetrate deeply into the nature of evil, but only the transfigured one can do this with authority. He must expect destruction for his enterprise, but on this destruction rests the world's redemption.

16

The Triumph of Evil

At midday a darkness fell over the whole land, which lasted till three in the afternoon; and at three Jesus cried aloud, "Eli, Eli, lema sabachthani?" which means, "My God, my God, why hast thou forsaken me?" (Mark 15: 33-34)

DEATH COMES TO all of us. To those who are thoughtful, this prospect comes to be seen increasingly as a merciful release from the unceasing toil of the world and the mounting decrepitude of the body. To those who are spiritually aware, death is the portal of entry to a fuller life in which much that we cannot understand in our present place of vantage may at last be opened to our comprehension and where we may see a little more clearly. To some death comes at the close of a long eventful life when the body's functions finally fail. To others the advent of death is abrupt, like an unwelcome intruder impinging himself at the peak of a useful, promising life and summarily calling the participant to a distant realm of unknown quality, far removed from his present surroundings. Death is at once man's friend and also his judge and accuser. It brings destruction with it and a termination of a life that may have been supremely worthwhile, for its summons is final.

But death is not to be equated with crucifixion, although some types of death are experiences of crucifixion. Crucifixion is the destruction of an innocent victim by a savagely evil impulse which has triumphed over the forces of light and compassion. The heart of the tragedy of crucifixion is the manifest triumph of the spirit that denies over the Spirit of God who affirms life and brings man closer to the divine image implanted within him. Until a person has seen and experienced the domination of evil, life-denying power over the warmth of love in personal sacrifice, he has not fully tasted of life. As I have already observed, there is nothing more terrible to behold than the manifest triumph of evil over good.

The evil of which I speak is not the impersonal inroads that a fatal malady makes in the life of a young person so that his promise is thwarted before it has had time to blossom fully. Neither is it the indifferent natural disasters that bring destruction to vast populations for no apparent reason. Jesus Himself observed that the eighteen people who were killed when the tower fell on them at Siloam were in no way more guilty than all the other people living in Jerusalem. Those who had died had, we believe, a new existence to experience, but those who were left were given time for repentance. (Luke 13: 4-5) Inasmuch as we all have partaken of the selfishness that rules the world, we must also be prepared to taste the evil that comes from this sinful participation. What we call retribution, or what the Hindu-Buddhist tradition knows as "karma", has a communal as well as an individual component. Indeed it has cosmic reverberations, for the psychic dimension is so interpenetrating in its intimacy that nothing we do or think leaves us without making its impact on the deeper core of the world, whose sensitivity is continuous with our own. When misfortune comes to us, we cry out: "Why did this have to happen to me?", as if we by virtue of our self-esteemed innocence did not deserve such a blow. We have forgotten the communal component.

There is, in fact, very little place for innocence in a world where selfishness is of the very order of communal life. Well did the Psalmist write: "In iniquity I was brought to birth and my mother conceived me in sin." (Psalm 51:5) This does not, of course, suggest that the act of procreation is evil, but that the soul when it incarnates into matter is immediately enclosed in a dense psychic atmosphere of sin. This sinfulness is not a particular judgement on the parents of the child, who may well be fine people intent on preserving the purity of family life and surrounding their children with an environment of true religion, as we most certainly believe the parents of Jesus did. It is rather a sober commentary on the world at large into which the child must inevitably take his place when he has outgrown the parental tutelage. If he is of the calibre of a normal person, the temptations to self-gratification and the ambitions of material success will, to greater or lesser extent, prevail, and his inner character will be to some degree marred and corrupted. If he were of the stature of Jesus, the insidious inroads of personal temptation would have no effect on his inner life, because he would be at one with the Father. But even, and indeed especially, if he remains truly innocent — and this true, tested innocence in the face of the world's temptation to attain personal power at the expense of others is to be contrasted with the immature, untested innocence of a child who has had no opportunity of experiencing such temptation — the full power of the world's stain and corruption will be raised against him. Indeed, it has to be so, because such a person is of the stature of a saint, and anyone aspiring to sanctification must confront the dark evil which denies, corrupts and destroys.

It would seem then that the answer to the question of why a particular person should be the victim of a misfortune is three-fold. Firstly, no one is exempt from bearing his share of the burden of the sin of the world. Secondly every misfortune borne with courage strengthens the character and gives one invaluable insights into the nature of reality. The last part of the answer is relevant only to the truly saintly person who has, in his quest for the vision of God, implicitly undertaken to bear the sin of the world; no one can know God before he has known every aspect of mortal suffering and degradation, as Jesus did. But to gain this ultimate knowledge, one has to enter the cloud of unknowing, and this means being prepared to lose contact with every article of faith that had previously sustained one in one's spiritual life. The ordeal of Job resulted in his personal enlightenment; the martyrdom of Jesus brought with it the enlightenment of the world. But neither the fictional Job nor the historical Jesus knew this when they were at the peak of their agony, even if they might possibly have been able to expound it intellectually to others at an earlier part of their ministry. This is the mystery of crucifixion.

There are, as we have already noted, two manifestations of God's transfiguring work in the world: the downward thrust of the Holy Spirit from the spiritual plane, through the psychical, to the material world, and the upward ascent of the Holy Spirit awake and vibrant in an aspiring soul. The point of contact is the hard, opaque, separative existence of men in a world of gravity unenlightened by grace. "The light shines on in the dark, and the darkness has never mastered it." (John 1:5) But the darkness has no intention of submitting to the light. Unredeemed man prefers his petty world of sensual gratification, mean, materialistic ambition, and selfish exploitation of his fellows to the spiritual world of freedom and self-abandonment to the providence inherent in the present moment. He will resist, to the death of his natural disposition, any attempt to shift him from the present situation of comfort and ease in which he finds himself. And yet he must be moved from the illusory world of safety and complacency to the realm of growth and experience, if he is to remain alive. The unfathomed psychic residue that darkens the universe has accrued from unresolved, unredeemed demonic activity, by which I mean actions performed by unenlightened beings, whether human or angelic, for selfish motives, to the exclusion of full, universal participation.

Thus we have the vertical flow of the Holy Spirit, downwards and upwards like the movement of the angels that Jacob saw in his vision of the ladder, which rested on the ground with its top reaching to heaven. (Genesis 28:12) And there is the horizontal barrier of uncomprehending material substance which blocks the power of that spiritual light by its opacity and inertia. This is symbolised by the Cross, on which the spiritual has to be sacrificed for the redemption of the material. And yet, were it not for this material barrier, the spiritual would remain unmanifest in the world of forms, the world that is to become perfect through the transfiguration of matter to Spirit. In other worlds, the dark incomprehension of the material world which is interpenetrated by the negative psychic forces that emanate from the "superhuman forces of evil in the heavens" (Ephesians 6:12), is not only the accuser of the light, its challenger, and its potential destroyer. It is also the way by which that light may finally experience itself in the world of forms and know itself also in the fellowship of created things. Perhaps even God learned something of His own nature when His Word incarnated and took on the tragic form of a crucified man. To be God is beyond our understanding in the glory and majesty of deity; to be man is limiting and humiliating in the transience and mortality that is the burden of humanity.

In the great confrontation between the life that affirms and the life that denies, between the power that lifts up the world to God and the power that erases, disintegrates, and reduces the world to nothing, between the person who moves towards the realisation of the divinity within him and the person who affirms the bestiality deeply set in the bodily consciousness, it is decreed that the lesser must have its time of triumph over the greater. This is the unbearable tragedy of mortal life. We, in our earthly consciousness, work with all goodwill towards the triumph of justice, righteousness, and understanding. And yet, as I have previously shown, each advance in what we call civilisation brings with it a necessary reaction, for man can never be satisfied with a purely worldly utopia. The boredom inherent in such a state of benign inertia would almost necessarily bring in its wake warfare and internecine strife. Indeed, the assertive drive innate in all normal people must be given its due; if it cannot be realised in creative work or sustaining relationships, it will rapidly be deflected to self-indulgence and then perverted to frankly anti-social activity. A worldly utopia in which a quiescent population lacked nothing for its material comfort but had no deeper reality to confront and explore would soon become as intolerable to contemplate as the heaven portrayed in popular versions of the religions of the world, in which a state of self-satisfaction is attained in a realm in which nothing of real moment ever seems to happen.

The reason for all this is that man was not made to live forever on this earth; at most it is a temporary abode where, in the limitation of a time-space universe, he may work out his salvation in the school of suffering, thereby coming to a fuller understanding of his own nature. Nor was man meant for the psychic realm. This too, after many spectacular episodes, comes finally to a dead-end which is bounded by the mirror of glamour casting its diverting reflections on all who gaze upon it. Neither worldly ambition nor psychic powers are able to transcend the limitation of the ego. On the contrary, they affirm it subtly and unobtrusively, no more dangerously than when the individual is full of good intentions, believing he is doing good and being of help to others. As the personal self is inflated, so the spiritual self recedes into the background. It can play its full role only when the person dedicates himself to service in the world of a type that brings no acclaim with it, and cultivates the practice of prayer.

"Miserable creature that I am, who is there to rescue me out of this body doomed to death?" (Romans 7:24) St Paul's cry comes from the heart of all men and indeed from the soul of the universe itself. Who can deliver the creation from the death that invades life and cuts off its meaning, from the darkness that triumphs over the light of aspiration, from the self-concern that imprisons people in a private world of selfish loneliness? St Paul answers: "God alone, through Jesus Christ our Lord." And the way in which this is attained is by submission to the darkness that ends in death, by forming a relationship that binds together even those whose vision is limited to material self-aggrandisement. The end of the life of a truly Spirit-filled person is the confrontation with the dark inertia of creation that resists change, and in this resistance is carried passively back to the chaos that existed before God breathed His Spirit on the darkness. The darkness too is divine, for everything that exists comes from God, but it is undifferentiated darkness, sometimes equated with the nothing out of which God created the universe. (2 Maccabees 7:28) The divine indwelling in all things ensures that there is nothing that does not come from God or is apart from Him. But there is a hierarchy of values, a gradation of glory which has been achieved by mankind working in the closest collaboration with the Holy Spirit. From the primal darkness, there has arisen a world civilisation presided over by the great spiritual geniuses of mankind, in whom the Spirit dwelt demonstrably. They have bequeathed the light of the Spirit to their followers, most of whom have dissipated it, but a few of whom have allowed it to kindle their own souls, so that they could in turn transmit it to those who followed them. And each in whom the light has truly shone, has added his contribution to the resurrection of the world. Many of these geniuses of the Spirit were able to live in some degree of compatibility with their surroundings, and they died in peace. But others had to take on themselves the burden of martyrdom.

Martyrdom in its spiritual context is never assumed by an act of personal will. It is forced on the saint by circumstances beyond his control. Willed martyrdom merges imperceptibly into exhibitionism on the one hand and suicide on the other. No wonder we should pray not to be brought to the test, for this is the test: to wrestle with the evil of the world in the assurance that the evil will prevail over the claims of the self, which has been purified, indeed transfigured, in the course of long and arduous service to the world. If the sacrifice of self has undertones of resentment, on the one hand, or of assurance, on the other hand, that the future — whether here or in the life beyond death — will see the victory of good over evil so that the evil is finally routed, overcome and destroyed, that sacrifice will lead to such hatred on its own behalf that the forces of evil will gain a victory undreamed of by the self-appointed martyr.

In the experience of crucifixion that marks the peak of spiritual attainment in this world, the one who enters this most fearsome ordeal must have left behind any concern for success in the work ahead of him. He must also have put away the natural personal preferences for his brethren that divide them into the favoured and the unfavoured, the liked and the disliked. True love, so searching that few could bear its full impact, goes beyond the affection we hold for those who are dear to us. Indeed, it must, if necessary, lower them, as Jesus did His brothers and mother on one occasion (Mark 3: 31-35), while it exalts the indifferent crowds of stricken people to fellowship with them. In this way, the aspirant leaves behind an immature type of value judgement based on the fruits of his actions, and also a private world of limited personal attachments. What is even more important is that he must also have ceased to hate the evil of the world. Instead he must feel compassion for all things; this is the fruit of identifying himself with all manner of sentient beings in the world — the corrupt and unclean no less than the noble and pure. This all-embracing compassion must take the place of anxious concern that the forces of right should triumph over those of wrong — as if we can properly judge what is right or wrong in so many of the world's dilemmas. Furthermore, this compassion is no longer an identification with the wretched of the earth in the comfortable security of a private existence. It is, on the contrary, a personal humiliation, so that one takes on, both to the outer gaze of hostile spectators and to one's inner consciousness all the attributes of the poor, the prisoner, the blind and the broken. The saving work of the spiritually anointed one, prophesied in Isaiah 61:1 and proclaimed by Jesus (Luke 4:18), finds its full and final fulfilment in the Passion of Christ. The healer of others cannot be healed Himself; the one Who showed men the way to heaven is excluded Himself; the bringer of abundant life is drained of life on a Cross that symbolises the intersection of the spiritual and the worldly with the manifest triumph of the worldly. This tragedy was no new event in Jesus' time, and it has not ended, not even two thousand years later.

There is a tendency amongst many contemporary thinkers to emphasise the Resurrection at the expense of the Crucifixion. While the Resurrection is certainly the central fact of the

Christian faith and cannot be proclaimed too often or too joyfully, it must be remembered that the Crucifixion which preceded it bore no certainty of a full resurrection of the slain one. Since all men rise from the dead into some type of after-life existence, it is not to be wondered at that Jesus also rose. But what did, on that occasion, rise from the dead, and how did that resurrection set in motion the resurrection of the universe?

Martyrdom has unfortunately been the lot of man since human consciousness first expressed itself. Our own century has seen enough martyrs viciously destroyed to make one despair of the triumph of God, as indeed one might be obliged to do were it not for the perfect sacrifice made by one Man. We cannot tell what attitude of mind prevailed amongst the world's martyrs. Some were, we may imagine, filled with hatred against their persecutors, while others looked for the ultimate triumph of what they believed. But how many were filled with charity to those that destroyed them? How many could flow out in love even to the power that denies? There was at least One who could pray to His Father (and our Father too) to forgive His destroyers, for they were blind and did not understand what they were doing. The great and unattainable teaching of the Sermon on the Mount — unattainable to those who live in the world of separation — at last rings true in this final confrontation: "Do not set yourself against the man who wrongs you. If someone slaps you on the right cheek, turn and offer him your left...Love your enemies and pray for your persecutors...Your heavenly Father makes his sun rise on good and bad alike, and sends the rain to the honest and the dishonest...There must be no limit to your goodness, as your heavenly Father's goodness knows no bounds." (Matthew 5: 38-48)

This attitude is not one of determined harmlessness, even in the face of intolerable provocation, which finds its modern counterpart in the questionable ideological position of non-violence and pacifism. I say it is questionable because experience teaches us that people who proclaim a non-violent, pacific approach to life are all too often violent

inwardly and not at peace with themselves. The point I made
in a previous section about the inadvisability of adopting too
austere a style of life before one is spiritually ready should be
remembered, for it applies also to the non-violent ethic. A
great deal of inner work under the guidance of the Spirit has
to be undertaken before the assertiveness of the self, which is
as much a part of the personality as the drives to procreation
or to spiritual understanding, can be diverted from violent
reactions that follow personal affronts to a more constructive,
compassionate way of life. There is more love in confronting
another person in conscious enmity than in evading a real
relationship by covering one's emotional sensibility with a
layer of assumed kindness that serves only to separate oneself
from him. Such an attitude is in fact mere condescension.
One is so inwardly sure of the rectitude of one's own position
that one will not consciously even hear what the other person
has to say. The one who loses most in this transaction is the
person who prides himself on his understanding. Those who
are wise learn more from difficult encounters than from the
writings of the learned.

The attitude of Jesus on the Cross was more than mere
acceptance and forgiveness. It was one of identification. The
"seven last words from the Cross" preached during the three
hours on Good Friday to commemorate the period when
darkness fell over the whole land and enveloped Jesus in
intolerable gloom, may well be apocryphal in context as well
as in sequence. But of one 'word' I have no doubt, because it
is so damaging to the witness of those Christians who cannot
face the implications of Jesus' full humanity: "My God, my
God, why has thou forsaken me?" It comes from Psalm 22,
and has been recited by Jews undergoing martyrdom
throughout the ages. Even if the complete obfuscation of
divine consciousness implicit in these words is thereby
softened, the fact that Jesus had to repeat the Psalms to
assuage His agony speaks fully of His human identity and His
participation in the gloom, dread and intolerable doubt of
all those confronting death, especially when their particular
mission seems to be doomed. And the end of that particular

three hours was one of doom. Silence prevailed. It is important to understand this, lest we relax too easily into the welcome Resurrection, as if it were a foregone conclusion right from the beginning of Jesus' ministry. Death had triumphed over life; man's fear and jealousy had killed God's gift to mankind. Once more a glorious hope for humanity was proved by the cynics to be yet another delusion.

The Spirit had buried Himself so deeply in the darkness of the uncomprehending earth that His light appeared to have been finally extinguished. The new gift of the Spirit was the ability to take on every vice and perversion, every stain and disfigurement that had disgraced the history of the world, that made men blanch in horror. And so He descended into Hell while the light appeared to have failed. And the good men rejoiced.

17

Peace

So he came and proclaimed the good news: peace to you who were far off, and peace to those who were near by. (Ephesians 2:17)

THE STRUGGLE IS over, and silence covers the darkness of the void. Widening ripples extend over the waters of oblivion. Sleep born of exhaustion and resignation to the night that must fall after day closes envelops mankind. "While daylight lasts we must carry on the work of him who sent me; night comes, when no one can work. While I am in the world I am the light of the world." (John 9: 4-5) Jesus said that when He was flesh of our flesh, but now He is no longer of our substance. Even the polarities of good and evil have been reconciled in a stillness where no new knowledge can be added. Sleep comes to all living forms as God's supreme gift of mercy, that the anxiety and the struggle for existence may be assuaged for a brief moment, and the creature may return to the region whence he originally came and whither he is ultimately to return.

Jonah slept in a corner of a ship before he was to face the consequences of his disobedience to the call of God. Jesus slept in a boat before He was to awaken and still the angry wind and sea, so that a dead calm prevailed. In the story of Jonah, nothing less than the prophet's self-sacrifice to the sea will ensure that the storm abates. In the life of Jesus, His very presence calms the elements, but it does not calm men, for

the One whom we call the Prince of Peace told His disciples
that He had not come to bring peace to the earth, but a
sword. He had come to set members of a family against each
other, so that each roof would be divided against itself. It is
evident that nature is restored to peace and harmony far
more readily than is man, who has been given dominion over
nature.

Before peace can come to mankind, each person must know
exactly who he is and what he stands for. This was what Jesus
effected in the lives of all who came into contact with Him.
The traditionally good were shown to harbour a cess-pit of
unclean desires within them; the pariahs of society discovered
a well of aspiration and love deeply hidden beneath a shoddy,
lust-ridden exterior. Thus the sinful tax-gatherer who had
faced his inner corruption and fought the inner battle before
God went home acquitted of his sins — and the home he
went to was not merely his earthly abode, but also his
heavenly destination; he had found peace. The self-righteous
religionist found no peace, and was intent on destroying the
One who threatened the uneasy equilibrium on which his life
was poised. The sword that Jesus brought with Him exposed
the polarities of good and evil unequivocally but also in a
light not previously dreamed of by the conventional moralist.

It was inevitable too that He should, in the end, fall victim
to that sword. Thus the Divine Man is the enemy of the
worldly good men, and in His death and descent, He is
aligned with and united to the outcast and the sinner. But are
the traditionally good, the upholders of moral rectitude and
the observers of religious rites, now to be cast into hell, and
the sinners of yesterday to be raised up to heaven? The
sentimentalist in us might affirm this judgement, but if we
were to abide by it, we would simply be returning to another
form of the fundamental polarity between darkness and light,
between evil and good. The participants may have changed
sides, but the action continues. The one quality lacking in
this approach is forgiveness, an attitude deficient also in our
own generation as much in those who fight for social justice as
in those who repress their fellow human beings because of

fear. It is not difficult to forgive those who have sinned, because they are weak; the weak are lovable and it is a joyous event when they are brought back into the family fold. It is more difficult to forgive the strong, those whose moral rectitude and legal propriety are beyond reproach, but whose lack of imagination and rigidity of attitude have separated them from their brethren and isolated them in a web of pride that prevents them receiving love. "Father, forgive them; they do not know what they are doing."

The foolishness of God does not come to reinstate the old principle of goodness and to attest the triumph of righteousness, but to bring together the shattered seeds of humanity in a community beyond good and evil, and where righteousness has been transfigured in love. This is the great difference between the prophetic call of the old dispensation which led the people back to God, and the proclamation of the new dispensation which sets in each soul the seal of God incarnate, a divinity previously hidden but now at last moving to its own manifestation.

We have seen that crucifixion means the manifest triumph of evil that kills the power of good in an earthly setting. The Spirit, previously merely incarnate in matter, has now buried Himself so inextricably in it that He appears to have been obliterated by it. Darkness has overcome the power of light, as it did during the final three hours of the Crucifixion. Then all is silent. On the third day He rose from the dead, and showed Himself in a new form to His brethren, none of whom recognised Him immediately. He was changed, and had the appearance of a stranger. Indeed, He always was a stranger. When Peter, in his agony, three times denied knowing the man, he was speaking a greater truth than he understood. Though Christ had dwelt some three years in the midst of the disciples, he was still a stranger among them. How could a person with such great powers of mind, soul and spirit, be other than a stranger to the very ordinary cross-section of humanity that the disciples represented! When He re-appeared, it was as if He were the gardener outside the tomb or a fellow traveller on the road to Emmaus. And

furthermore He was these people and all others also in
addition to being His glorified self. For in Him it is now
possible for each member of the human race to attain, in his
own life, what He showed in the practice of the common life.

Resurrection is the other side of desolation; it is the
reconciliation of all discordant elements into a new creation
whose nature is peace. The risen Christ speaks of peace in the
voice of peace. He tells Mary of Magdala not to cling to Him,
not to touch Him any more, for He is no longer the mortal
Jesus incarcerated by the attitudes and judgements of her
world, which was His world also. The past is indeed over, the
sword has been destroyed, and the way of confrontation has
been transfigured in an all-embracing love that includes all
opposites and binds them in a whole which does each full
justice and yet transforms them into the fullness of their
integrity.

In His life Jesus demonstrated both the miraculous powers
and transcendent wisdom of the Word of God and the humiliation and suffering of the least of men. He had in His life
reconciled these two final polarities. By identifying Himself
with the common criminal up to the fact of death on the
Cross, He identified Himself with the Father in a more
perfect way than at any previous point in His ministry. "In
the days of his earthly life he offered up prayers and petitions,
with loud cries and tears, to God who was able to deliver him
from the grave. Because of his humble submission his prayer
was heard: son though he was, he learned obedience in the
school of suffering, and, once perfected, became the source of
eternal salvation for all who obey him, named by God high
priest in the succession of Melchizedek." (Hebrews 5: 7-10)

In this reconciliation there is a change in both the elements
of Jesus. The tortured body has been freed from the physical
law of decay, death and corruption to the spiritual law of
eternal life. It has transcended the limits cast by time and
space, and has attained the spiritual qualities of omnipre-
sence and omnipotence; it can never be destroyed, and is
among all who are gathered together in His name (which
means all those who have sacrificed the lower nature

of selfish concern for the greater love of the brethren). The soul, assuredly always one with the Father in dedication and intent, is now fully one with Him in the identity of love: this full flow of love is the seal of the perfection Jesus attained through obedience in the school of suffering. "God was in Christ reconciling the world to himself, no longer holding men's misdeeds against them." (2 Corinthians 5:19) And Jesus, in His fully human stature, is raised to the perfect knowledge of love.

Spiritual warfare is never won decisively either in the world of matter or the psychical realms of discarnate spirits. The end of Jesus' life is failure, at least in terms of overcoming the powers of darkness by deliberate confrontation. The victory of uncreated light over darkness is attained by the broken Christ, when He has only His complete failure to confront. The power of God's love emerges fully at this moment, and Jesus can accept all conditions of men and all manner of circumstances, the good and the bad, as His companions. Judgement and condemnation are finally superseded by an acceptance of things as they are, and at once the love that is in the dying Christ can break through into the lives of all who are willing to accept Him for what He is — both God's representative on earth and a loathsome criminal — and let that love start the process of their own healing. Gone is the Jesus who castigated the lawyers and Pharisees so fiercely during His ministry (Matthew 23) and drove out the traders from the Temple precincts (Mark 11: 15-19) — and thereby set in motion a hostility between future generations of His followers and those from whose stock He Himself was born, a hostility which only after two thousand years of terrible hatred and frequent persecution is being finally healed as both sides learn something of the reality that He came to know during the last hours of His earthly life and when He had descended into Hell. There He went so that He could set in motion the liberation of souls imprisoned in hatred, resentment, and fear by proclaiming the gospel of reconciliation: that God accepts people as they are, and by, in turn, accepting God's supreme invitation to share His table, they may leave their prison and enter the liberty of the eternal realm whose nature is love.

It is fortunate that the Church has never held absolutely to any one theory of the Atonement. The doctrine is crucial to an understanding of the purpose of the Incarnation, but its full import is beyond intellectual analysis; it has to be realised in the life of each believer. In essence it means that when one "knows" Christ, one is set free from the thralldom of sin and its wages of death. When God comes to us in a form that knows us through participating in the full, fearsome business of being a man, and by coming to us, shows His full acceptance of us as we now stand — we can accept the love that flows from Him — His very energy as it were — and be changed by it. This change sets in motion a complete awakening of the person which culminates in his own deification, the crucial stage of which is mystical transfiguration. Once Christ is known, the claims of the personal self recede into the background of our lives, and the work for the coming of the Kingdom takes priority.

It must be said, however, that this encounter with the humiliated, risen, triumphant Christ (the three are one) is not a once-for-all event. We grow progressively into the knowledge of His love. Thus the young Christian tends to be full of judgement against the sins of the world. He soon begins to doubt the integrity of many ordained ministers of the faith who may show what he regards as a dangerous ambivalence towards the dark side of humanity. To him black and white are eternally separate with a great gulf set between them, and he will have no difficulty in finding texts from the Gospel to substantiate this point of view. But as he grows in the knowledge of the love of God and in the knowledge of the chaos that prevails inside himself, so he will be able to identify Christ not only with the transcendent God, but also with suffering humanity. As he is able to take this great step downwards, so God will lift him upward, and he too will become an instrument for raising the world from sinful self-abandon to the abandonment of the self, to the service of others and to God. The Christ of the Resurrection was indeed a changed person. I believe, as I have already said, that His body was, while the same in essence as He had used when He was alive in the flesh, also completely different; the risen Christ, though identical in person with the crucified Jesus, is also different from Him. His physical appearance was so changed that His friends did not recognise Him until He had made some gesture that brought with it a deeper identification. The change, presaged at the time of transfiguration when the body became transparent to the light of God, was completed in the spiritual transformation of the resurrection body.

Of even greater import, however, is the spiritual radiance that emanates from the risen Christ. He is now fully at peace, eternally so; indeed, He is "the peace of God that passes all understanding". "Peace is my parting gift to you, my own peace, such as the world cannot give," (John 14: 27) is a text from Jesus' farewell discourses, but it applies much more perfectly to the blessing that the risen Christ said when He broke bread with the apostles on the way to Emmaus. He comes to them unobtrusively as a stranger on the road, imperceptibly enters the conversation until He commands it, then lifts up the hearts of the broken, bereft apostles. But only when He stays to break bread with them and says the blessing, do they know Him. Then He vanishes from their sight. (Luke 24: 13-32) A new Christ had appeared in the person of the man Jesus: at peace, glowing with suffused joy, beyond the polarities of good and evil, no longer condemning even the actions and attitudes of the hypocrites of religion. He has forgiven all those who have betrayed Him, not so much in recorded words as in the deep underlying compassion.

Jesus instructs the same disciple who denied knowing Him on three occasions to feed the lambs and sheep of the new dispensation. But first He enquires gently but perceptively whether Peter's affection has returned. Poor Peter, the true representative of Everyman, breaks down as he confronts the enormity of his own betrayal of his Master. Jesus, however, utters no word of reproach. Instead He speaks of the service Peter is to offer in the future and the martyrdom he is destined to suffer in the name of Him whom he now fervently affirms. Peter himself had undergone a lesser resurrection and had emerged a changed, but by no means perfect man. His future life as an apostle of Christ was to wear away the ambivalence in his own nature between self-defence on the one hand and total commitment to his fellow men on the other, so that the image of God within his own soul could become cleansed and radiant.

The resurrected Christ blesses the world in love, a love that knows no bounds. In union with Him, He is as a garment in the folds of which Jew and Greek, slave and freeman, male and female have moved beyond the divisions set by men and nature, and are now one person. (Galatians 3: 27-28) In the same way, the light and the darkness, the good and the evil of this world, are taken up into Him and are transformed into a new light, which is beyond the creation and the very outflowing energy of the Godhead. The triumph of love means the transfiguration of the whole created universe so that it follows the way of ascent shown by the body of Jesus. And this transfiguration must include all beings, those whom the world calls bad no less than the acclaimed good, the unjust as well as the just. What the world calls good is the pattern of divine creation in the divided realm of time and space, while evil is the tendency to revert to past attitudes of isolation, separation, and destruction that have their end in the primal chaos before the Word of God summoned the world out of the void. Were it not for the constant interplay of these two elements, nothing would ever happen, and there would be a state of inertia in which the creation would sleep, in an unending heaven of dull complacency. That would be a real hell.

Neither the evil nor the good of this world has a primary, substantive reality; while the one creates and fashions new works in a transient world, the other denies, degrades, and disintegrates. Both are aspects of the energy man acquired from God, when he came to a knowledge of his own separative existence at that period of development known theologically as "the Fall". This primal energy, which is of the Holy Spirit, was then bestowed on man for the exercise and development of his own free will; when used selfishly and apart from the greater life of the world, it becomes perverted and demonic, contaminating the psychic atmosphere. The same energy used constructively and selflessly, however, produces a blessing of warmth, encouragement and enlightenment in the psychic realm, which leaves its record in the lives of future generations of sentient beings.

Both aspects of this energy are deeply placed in the soul of man; in psychological terms, they represent the shadow and the higher, spiritual self respectively. In many people the shadow side seems to dominate over the inner Christ of the higher self to such an extent that one may be tempted to despair of their redemption from the darkness to the light. And yet these same people can show themselves capable, in exceptional circumstances, of a gesture of such self-sacrifice, even on behalf of a stranger, that Christ Himself could hardly surpass it in nobility and love. Conversely, how many of those who fondly believe they are on the spiritual path and speak knowledgeably about deep and difficult matters, betray themselves day by day when they fail to show love and understanding in the course of some minor situation in their own lives!

It seems that evil and suffering are as integral to life on earth as are beauty and goodness. All working together create the environment in which the sentient creature — who, in our world, is man, for he alone appears to have the moral and intellectual capacity to distinguish between good and evil — can attain to his full stature. Mankind knows the measure of this stature: its saints in all the great religious traditions and especially the known and yet woefully unknown Jesus Christ, Who combined in His one person the perfection of the Godhead and the lowliness of the criminal on the scaffold. In Him good and evil find a common place of refuge, and, by submitting to the evil of the world, He changes both the face of evil and of good. From being perpetually opposed to one another, in irreconcilable enmity, they now flow together in a new stream. The energy of the Holy Spirit given to man by

God, so that he might work out his own salvation through the experience of life and the experiment of relationships (not only with people but with the entire creation) is now re-united in purpose. The evil impulse is won by love to a new understanding of reality, while the good impulse is perfected by love to accept the evil as part of itself, and to move beyond judgement to mercy, beyond the demands of righteousness to self-transcending forgiveness.

"Then he showed me the river of the water of life, sparkling like crystal, flowing from the throne of God and of the Lamb down the middle of the city's street. On either side of the river stood a tree of life, which yields twelve crops of fruit, one for each month of the year; the leaves of the tree serve for the healing of the nations. Each accursed thing shall disappear. The throne of God and of the Lamb will be there, and his servants shall worship him; they shall see him face to face, and bear his name on their foreheads. There shall be no more night, nor will they need the light of lamp or sun, for the Lord God will give them light; and they shall reign for evermore." (Revelation 22: 1-5)

The glorious Holy City, the New Jerusalem seen in the vision of the writer of the Book of Revelation, needs no temple, for its temple is the sovereign Lord God and the Lamb. It needs no sun or moon to shine upon it, for God's glory (His emergent light) gives it light, and its lamp is the Lamb. The one discordant note is the exclusion of anything unclean or of anyone whose ways are false or foul (Revelation 21: 22-27). In fact the City of God must, by the very nature of His love for all His creation, be able to accept the unclean as well as the clean, and find room even for the false and the foul. But in the transfiguring light of the Lamb, who brought together the world's evil and its good into a new relationship, both are changed and raised to the glory of God, so that in truth "each accursed thing shall disappear." As the mystics have known, there is a spark of God in even the most degraded object. He who can have sufficient love to bless that object, liberates the spark from within it and ensures its glorification. There is nothing beyond redemption in creation;

there is only that which has not yet been made holy. This is man's supreme duty and privilege. It is the heart of the ministry of healing.

The great mystics knew well when they said that God was beyond good and evil. Both of these polarities are subject to the world of change, decay, death and rebirth. God transcends polarities; in Him all contradictions coincide; in Him there is no duality. We come to Him when we are freed from the law of change by leaving behind the desire for judgement of others and entering the unitary way of love. This love, however, can come to us in its fullness only when we have trodden the path of sacrifice and have been crucified on the cross of material inertia and spiritual aspiration. When we have been shriven of the last vestige of personal clinging so that our very self has been presented as a sacrifice on the altar of truth, only then can we pass beyond the bondage of material illusion and know the truth that has set us free. Only then can we really know ourselves, for we will have seen God, and know that union with Him is reality. So it follows that no one can know God until he has died; every little death of one's present preconceptions and certainties is a birth into a greater authenticity of being. The death of personality inevitably precedes the resurrection of the person into a new creation, at one with all things and with them in union with God.

The resurrection of the person cannot proceed as an isolated event. It has cosmic dimensions. The release of the whole created universe from the law of change and death to the eternal glory of "uncreated nature" — the plan of perfection in the divine mind which existed before the creature disrupted it by the selfish use of his God-given free will — is to be restored at the end of time when the creature has attained the stature of Christ. Cosmic redemption is the final purpose of the divine life in man.

The Creation story tells of the original harmony that prevailed between the animal kingdom and man, both of whom fed on plant life. (Genesis 1: 29-30) Enmity between the animals and man commences when man deserts the unitive life for a separative existence based on a divisive, selfish knowledge which is centred on a polarisation of good and evil — with man inevitably being attracted along the lesser path that leads to destruction. (Genesis 3:15) The break in relationship between man and animal life is complete when God invokes His new covenant with Noah by which "the fear and dread of man shall fall upon all wild animals on earth, on all birds of heaven, on everything that moves upon the ground and all fish in the sea; all are given into his hands." (Genesis 9:2)

We need not accept the literal historical accuracy of this account to be aware of the deep mythological truth that underlies it. Not only is man the great enemy of the animal kingdom (and indeed of the natural order by his selfish appropriation of its resources), but nature is in enmity against itself, the one creature fighting the other for its existence and sustenance. In contemporary society man has at last come to understand the inadequacy of his past stewardship of natural resources, and the work of conservation is now seen to be a most pressing priority for the future life of mankind on this planet. But even this welcome acknowledgment of responsibility for the conservation of nature's resources has strong undertones of selfishness. The concern is primarily for human survival; concern for nature itself is a very secondary factor, if indeed it exists at all.

St Paul, in one of his greatest flashes of illumination, saw matters in a very different light. "The sufferings at present endured are not to be compared with the splendour, as yet unrevealed, which is in store for mankind. The created universe waits with eager expectation for God's sons to be revealed. It was made the victim of frustration, not by its own choice, but because of him who made it so; yet always there was hope, because the universe itself is to be freed from the shackles of mortality and enter upon the liberty and splendour of the children of God." (Romans 8: 18-21) He goes on, in this great cosmic insight, to say that the universe at present groans as if in the pangs of childbirth, as those baptised in Christ, to whom the Spirit is given as first fruits of the harvest to come, also groan inwardly while they wait for God to make them His sons and set their whole body free. For they have been saved, although only in hope. Its fulfilment, when they actually see its establishment, is not with them yet; they have to wait for this, and in doing so, they show their endurance.

Indeed, only when man "has left self behind, taken up his cross and come on the life that is Christ" will he realise his salvation and move towards deification — becoming a realised son of God. He must no longer care for his own safety, for then he is lost. But if he will let himself be lost for Christ's sake and the good news of redemption, that man is safe. This basic teaching of Christ (in Mark 8: 34-36) is also the universal teaching of all the great religious traditions, and the path is a common one trodden by all their saints. It is the way of purification, directed by illumination, and consummated in union with God. And in unity with God, neither the animals nor the plants, nor indeed any atom of created matter is excluded. If one particle of substance is withheld, there is no salvation for even the holiest saint.

Isaiah, in his greatest messianic prophecy, describes how the gifts of the Spirit of God will rest on the Anointed One; wisdom and understanding, counsel and power, knowledge and the fear of the Lord. When He has come, peace and harmony will prevail once more between the animal kingdom and man; "They shall not hurt or destroy in all my holy mountain; for as the waters fill the sea, so shall the land be filled with the knowledge of the Lord." (Isaiah 11: 1-9) The Anointed One has come in the form of many great saints and prophets of old, supremely, the Christian would affirm, in the person of the Lord Jesus. But this prophecy will not be fulfilled until all human beings have been anointed by their own free choice and dedication to the will of God.

The great souls of the past have shown us the way, and in Christ are indeed the very way. But they cannot do the work for us. It is we whose duty and joy it is to assume their mantle and bring to completion what they have started.

The last recorded words of the Resurrected Christ were: "Follow me".

Epilogue

JESUS HAS LEFT us, but His resurrected body multiplies in blessing whenever bread is broken in His name. He is flesh of our flesh whenever we partake of the Eucharistic sacrament, because His body sanctifies every element of the created world when it is consecrated in His name. And so it is that the body which is now one with the Father in the unitary realm of eternity is also dissipated in the myriad atoms that compose the physical world and interpenetrate the psychic realm. His real presence is with mankind when we remember Him and call on His name in dedication and in love. Evil and good, the darkness and the light, have now been raised from the separative world where judgement and condemnation reign, to take their place in His mystical body.

Only when humanity has understood this truth and practised it in the world of separation and suffering, will death be swallowed up and victory be won, for "we shall be changed. The perishable being will be clothed with the imperishable and what is mortal clothed with immortality."